MW01234473

Grow Old Along with Me

Aging Gracefully in a Graceless Age

Mark S. Milwee

WESTBOW
P R E S S®
A DIVISION OF THOMAS NELSON
& ZONDERVAN

WestBow Press books may be ordered through booksellers or by contacting:

WestBow Press
A Division of Thomas Nelson & Zondervan
1663 Liberty Drive
Bloomington, IN 47403
www.westbowpress.com
1 (866) 928-1240

ISBN: 978-1-9736-4335-7 (sc)
ISBN: 978-1-9736-4334-0 (hc)
ISBN: 978-1-9736-4336-4 (e)

Library of Congress Control Number: 2018912492

Print information available on the last page.

WestBow Press rev. date: 10/19/2018

CONTENTS

This book is dedicated to my loving, funny, and multitalented wife, Amanda. You have stood by me now for over thirty years, and I look forward to our growing old together. My prayer is that we will grow old gracefully and be a blessing to those following along behind. I love you, and I know the best is yet to be ...

INTRODUCTION

I can't think of a better way to introduce this book than by sharing the opening stanza of one of my favorite poems. The poem was written by Robert Browning. It is titled, "Rabbi Ben Ezra."

> Grow old along with me!
> The best is yet to be,
> The last of life, for which the first was made:
> Our times are in his hand
> Who saith, "A whole I planned,
> Youth shows but half; trust God: see all, nor be afraid!"

I love the line where he says, "The last of life, for which the first was made."

I want to begin by confessing, I love senior adults. Now, before you toss this book aside and say, "Well, then, this book is not for me," let me explain why I believe this would be a big mistake. Currently 42.6 million people in the United States are sixty-five or older. This is remarkable when you consider at the turn of the twentieth century (just over one hundred years ago) only 3 million people in our country were in that category. However, what may be even more incredible than either of these two figures is that by the year 2030, 70 million people will be in this category, and by 2060 there will be ninety million seniors in America! It makes you want to go out and buy stock in Geratol or something!

One of my favorite sayings about aging is, "Getting older is really not all that bad when you consider the alternative!" I came across a quote that reminds me I'm getting older. It declared, "Every young man starts out in life expecting to find a pot of gold at the end of the rainbow; by middle age, most of them have at least found the pot!" But the person who said, "You're only as old as you feel right after you try to demonstrate how young you are," summed up best the real test of aging! It's just a fact of life that we are all getting older, and the church that taps into this growing population will be the church that succeeds in the twenty-first century.

The Bible has a lot to say about aging, and it gives us plenty of examples of men and women who served God faithfully until they reached a ripe old age. I think immediately of Abraham, Sarah, Moses, Joshua, Caleb, and, in the New Testament, John, Zechariah, Elizabeth, Simeon, and Anna. The Bible is full of individuals who served God faithfully all of their lives, illustrating that God is interested not just in how we start, but in how we finish in our Christian lives.

My desire in writing this book is to challenge you to see the valuable contributions the elderly make in the life of the church. I don't want to be tossed out on my ear when I reach a certain age. I want to faithfully serve the Lord all of my life and for the rest of my life. I believe we need to recapture the respect, honor, and dignity ascribed to the elderly in scripture. The admonition to respect your elders is not just a quaint saying from yesteryear. It is a prescription for the health and vitality of any church that understands the importance of valuing one of our most precious assets. Older men and women accomplished remarkable deeds in the pages of scripture. We need to learn from their examples and respect the elders God has placed in our lives. Grow old along with me! The best is yet to be—the last of life, for which the first was made.

CHAPTER ONE

━━━━━━━━━━━━━━━━━━━━━━━━━━━━━━

The Current Crisis

I enjoy reading the "Pickles" comic strip. I read one recently where two elderly men were sitting on a park bench and one was reading a newspaper. He turns to his friend and says, "Hmm, it says here surveys show that one-third of all retirees age 65 and older would prefer to still be working." His friend replies by saying, "Yeah. I know I would! I'd prefer my knees to still be working, my back, my eyes, my circulatory system ..."

But all joking aside, there is a grain of truth in this cartoon. Seniors who are committed to the Lord want to work and contribute and make a difference with their lives. They want to make an impact for the Lord all the days of their lives. Unfortunately, I've observed that in many respects, America is not the nicest place in the world in which to grow old. I say this because, in our country, so much emphasis is placed upon youth. We have a tendency to discard our older adults with all of their wisdom, ideas, and potential.

We experienced this in our immediate family over the course of the past decade. My father, who pastored numerous churches for over thirty-five years, was unable to find another place of ministry after he went through heart bypass surgery a few years ago. Everywhere he went, people told him they were looking for somebody younger who could appeal to the younger generation. My father-in-law experienced a similar situation. He lost his technology job just before retirement. Apparently, the company he had been loyal to for years didn't want to have to pay the retirement benefits. I clipped the following story out of the local newspaper over twenty years ago, because it struck a chord deep within me. It illustrates the tragic consequences of neglecting the elderly.

> Today, as I entered a fast food restaurant, there was a little old lady standing outside with a shopping cart. She had a dress on and the usual cobbler's apron over it, ready to preside over her kitchen, like thousands of other grandmothers all over the country. She looked up at me and asked if I could spare a little change, so she could "get a little something." I am a veteran of con artists. I spend much of my time in the inner city, and there are not too many stories I haven't heard. I know the local homeless and not so homeless, and I can spot a faker a mile away … This lady was in need. She stood quietly while I pulled out what I had, and as I handed her $3 she started to shake and cry. I hugged her and told her to go get what she could. She immediately went in and ordered the smallest hamburger and a coffee. She spent the next little while eating the hamburger and getting several refills of coffee … As she left, she came back smiling and said, "Thank you honey, I am saving the rest for dinner."[1]

The lady writing these words then closed with the following appeal:

---

[1] JoAnn Horton, Editorial, *The Argus*, 5 May 1995.

MARK S. MILWEE

I am a staunch supporter of reforming the welfare system, as I daily see gross abuse. But nowhere, nowhere in this great country of ours, should our grandmothers be hungry.[2]

I tend to agree. It's maddening when we neglect the needs of this growing population.

However, with this being said, I'll add that I've seen a number of new churches advertise their churches by saying, "This is not your grandma's church," or "Are you tired of traditional church?" or "A new church for a new day." I understand the message they are trying to communicate. They want people to know their church is young, hip, and exciting. However, when you launch your new work by alienating the seniors, or even worse, when you announce to a transitioning congregation, "We are moving in a new direction, and you seniors should find a new place to worship," you have just cut off your nose to spite your face. You have alienated a large and growing segment of the population who desperately love Jesus. You are hurting yourself by not taking into consideration all of the wonderful gifts, talents, and abilities senior adults bring to the table, not to mention the financial stability seniors bring to a church.

Ed Lewis, executive director of CE National, in an article titled, "Keeping Older Adults in the Church," writes about his concerns with how believers view older adults in the church today. He begins the article by highlighting numerous biblical reasons for pursuing younger people, but then he adds,

But here is what scares me. We are losing our older adults! We must honor older believers *and* we need to reach older people for Christ. In the USA there are more people over 50 than there are people under 18. Who is reaching the older people? Are

---

[2] Ibid.

we losing them? Are they becoming detached from the church? And on top of all that the Bible honors age, not youth. Job 12:12 says that "Wisdom is with the aged, and understanding in length of days." It also states that "young men must not rebuke an elder" (1 Timothy 5:1) and they are to "treat elderly women like mothers."[3]

I wholeheartedly agree. We have to find ways to incorporate senior adults into the life of the church. Charles Sell, in his book *Transitions through Adult Life*, shares,

> "From those who study the aged, the message is clear: They want to be involved. They often feel discriminated against when excluded from offices and positions because of age …What older adults want is to be integrated into the church's life."[4]

The church I most recently pastored in San Diego provided two opportunities for worship on Sunday mornings. The early service was traditional, with a choir, organ, and hymns. It appealed primarily to the senior adults. The second service was contemporary, with drums, band, guitars, and all the bells and whistles. It appealed primarily to the younger generation. Guess which service grew the most during my tenure at the church? This was in Southern California, in one of the trendiest places in America, but our early service grew on a consistent basis, while the later service struggled to attract and hold a crowd. I also did an analysis at one point and determined that almost 90 percent of our income was coming out of the traditional service. I'm not down on contemporary worship. I enjoyed the

---

[3] Ed Lewis, Keeping Older Adults in the Church," CE National, accessed 15 March 2018, https://www.cenational.org/resource/keep-older-adults-church.
[4] Charles Sell, *Transitions through Adult Life* (Grand Rapids: Zondervan Publishing House, 1991), p. 210.

second service. However, I'm trying to show the folly of alienating the senior adults in your community. Sure, it required extra time, energy, and effort to provide the additional service, but it also paid high dividends for the church.

Our traditional service grew for two reasons: First, we were one of only a few local options for seniors who wanted a more traditional service. It's getting harder and harder to find a more traditional service in many parts of the country. Sadly, many of our new members came from a nearby mega-church that told its members, many of whom had been at the church for over sixty years, that they needed to find a new place of worship. We did not actively seek these people, but many came because they heard through friends that we had something for them and that we valued seniors.

It's heartbreaking to sit with an elderly couple and hear them tell you that the church to which they have given the greater part of their lives didn't want them anymore. These were former leaders, deacons, and elders. They were not gossips or even trying to spread evil rumors about their previous church. They were heartbroken by this turn of events. We had the joy of welcoming many of them into our church family.

The second reason our church grew in this area is that we placed value upon senior adults. We didn't see them as second-class citizens who had outlived their effectiveness. We embraced them. We provided opportunities for leadership and participation. We provided opportunities for fellowship and growth. We valued their contributions, and we let them know we were proud to have them as part of our church family. Stephen Mattson, in an article titled, "Have Churches Abandoned the Elderly?" writes,

> It's easy to stereotype "old people" as complainers
> and people who are out of touch, but it's time to
> start honoring the elderly within our churches and

realizing that they have just as much value and
worth as everyone else—they are God's creation![5]

I hesitate to even share this, but I know the only appeal that can get the attention of some is money. A gentleman began to attend our church who was recently widowed. We made him feel welcome, included him in our activities, and treated him with dignity and respect.

After approximately a year of attending our services, he called and set up an appointment to meet with me, and it was during this meeting that he told me his story. It seems that he and his wife had been very active members in another local church for many years. Regrettably, his wife contracted cancer and suffered for over a year with many difficult procedures and hospital stays before her death. Although they had been very active in the previous church, no one came to visit with them or called to check on her during her long and protracted illness. As a result of this negligence, the first Sunday following her death was his first Sunday at our church.

He then shared with me how he had come into a great sum of money, and the desire of his heart was to give some of it to the church. I graciously thanked him for his kindness and generosity. He brought me a check later that week for $50,000. He also told me another $50,000 would be coming before the end of the year! This money should have and would have gone to the other church had someone taken the time to minister to him and his wife during their time of need. We did not welcome and embrace this man because we thought we might get money out of him one day. We had no idea he had this kind of money. We valued him as an individual of dignity and worth, and God rewarded our loving-kindness.

Does this story mean the same thing will happen to you and your church the moment you embrace senior adults? No, of course

---

[5] Stephen Mattson, "Have Churches Abandoned the Elderly?" *Sojourner's Magazine*, 23 October 2013, accessed March 15, 2018, https://sojo.net/article/have-churches-abandoned-elderly.

MARK S. MILWEE

not! But it is still the right and honorable thing to do. All people are precious in God's sight, including senior adults. They have wisdom, skill, and an eagerness to serve.

A few years ago, I had the privilege of attending a pastor appreciation luncheon where the speaker asked all the pastors in the room to stand. The crowd applauded, and then he asked everyone to sit down if they had been a pastor for one year or less. He had folks sitting down in five-year increments. When he got to twenty years or less, I was still standing and over half the room was already seated. I thought, *Wow, I must be getting older!* I've been a pastor now for over twenty years. If you add the years I spent in youth ministry, then I've been in full-time ministry for almost thirty years. I can hardly believe it has been that long, but it has been an interesting and rewarding experience.

I like what Paul proclaimed to the church in Philippians 3:13b-14: "Forgetting what lies behind and straining forward to what lies ahead, I press on toward the goal for the prize of the upward call of God in Christ Jesus." My prayer is that, with God's help, I will be able to press on for many more years. In fact, compared to the two men in the room who were still standing at the end of the time of recognition, I'm just getting started! Both men had been serving the Lord faithfully for over fifty years! I applaud them for their faithfulness, and I encourage you to continue living faithfully each and every day. I believe consistency over time is how the real growth occurs in our Christian lives.

Seniors have so much to offer, and since they have age and experience under their belts, they know where they are truly valued and appreciated. This doesn't mean they should be catered to and valued more than others in the congregation, but they should be respected and provided with opportunities for their voices to be heard. Here are a few suggestions to minister to senior adults more effectively:

1. Give senior adults opportunities to serve in meaningful ways in the church.
2. Treat the elderly with respect and dignity.
3. Find ways for seniors to minister to each other.
4. Encourage mentoring relationships between seniors and younger people.
5. Conduct intergenerational events.
6. Consider offering a worship service with a traditional approach.

Ed Lewis, the executive director of CE National, whom I quoted earlier, offers this wonderful advice:

> Love the older people …and mobilize them for service. They want to be involved in helping to make a difference! And if you honor them, let them be honored by allowing them to be seen in church. They are just as important as the other believers.[6]

The crisis, as I see it, is we have an ever-increasing population of senior adults, who are being pushed out of the church instead of embraced and valued. They have important and significant contributions to make. So the question we have to ask ourselves is, "Are we going to obey the word of God and respect our elders?" This is the subject of chapter 2.

---

[6] Ed Lewis, "Keeping Older Adults in the Church," CE National, accessed March 15, 2018, https://www.cenational.org/resource/keep-older-adults-church.

CHAPTER TWO

Respect Your Elders

The Bible is very specific about how we are to treat senior adults. We are clearly taught in God's word to treat older people with respect, dignity, and honor. For instance, the Bible declares in Leviticus 19:32, "You shall stand up before the gray head and honor the face of an old man, and you shall fear your God: I am the Lord."

And in the New Testament we read, "Do not rebuke an older man harshly, but exhort him as if he were your father. Treat younger men as brothers, older women as mothers, and younger women as sisters, with absolute purity" (1 Timothy 5:1–2).

Paul, writing to the younger Timothy, says in effect, "Treat the elderly as if they were your own parents!" Of course, this is where the problem begins for many people. They disrespect their parents when they are young, and then it carries over into adulthood. The first commandment with a promise says, "Honor your father and your mother, so that you may live long in the land the Lord your God is giving you" (Exodus 20:12).

God expects us to respect our elders. This is why we are told, "Honor the face of an old man, and don't rebuke an older man harshly." The word *rebuke* literally means, "Don't strike at an older man." Instead, encourage him as if he were your father. Therefore, we should treat the elderly with gentleness and respect.

I believe this admonition to treat the elderly with respect is a word that desperately needs to be spoken in our world today because, sadly, things are getting out of hand. A ninety-one-year-old friend and mentor of mine innocently answered a knock at the door one day. When he opened the door, armed men forced their way into his home and robbed him at gunpoint. The assailants beat my elderly friend so badly that he had to spend several days in the ICU of the local hospital. Not long after this incident, an elderly lady from our congregation was sitting and waiting for her son to pick her up for dinner. She left the door ajar to make it easier for her son to get in when he arrived, but again, unfortunately, someone rushed in and grabbed her purse, and rushed back out the door before she had time to even respond.

We have become a "throw-away" society when it comes to senior adults, but, just because you have reached a certain age, doesn't mean you are useless and have nothing of value to contribute. Senior adults have a wealth of knowledge, talents, and abilities. We are foolish when we refuse to recognize them. It is our responsibility as Christians to care for the elderly and treat them with respect, honor, and dignity. The Bible even goes so far as to indicate respecting the elderly is a sign of godliness. Notice how the text continues in 1 Timothy 5, verses 3–4:

> Honor widows who are truly widows. But if a widow has children or grandchildren, let them first learn to show godliness to their own household and to make some return to their parents, for this is pleasing in the sight of God.

Now drop down to verse 8 and notice the warning,

But if anyone does not provide for his relatives, and especially for members of his household, he has denied the faith and is worse than an unbeliever.

Did you know the Bible said this? This is the verse I couldn't get out of my mind when I was trying to make the life-altering decision to relocate my family from Southern California to Alabama to be closer to the widows in my family. The Bible says we put our religion into practice by caring for our immediate family, our parents, and our grandparents, and if we don't do this, we are denying the faith and are worse than an unbeliever. It is first and foremost our responsibility as Christians to care for our elders, and as we do this, the Bible says we are putting our faith into practice. This reminds me of a story about a lady and her mother who went to visit a retirement community. The daughter was hoping her mom would like the place and want to go there to live. So, as they were leaving, the daughter said, "People sure were having fun. When I'm their age, living here would be perfect!"

Her mother said, "That's great. When you get there, I'll come to visit you!"

I've spent more than my share of time at nursing homes, convalescent centers, and retirement communities. I served as a minister to senior adults in one of my first ministry assignments, and, of course, numerous seniors have attended all the churches I have pastored through the years. I'm not trying to make anyone feel guilty, if you've had to place one of your parents in such a place. From my experience, I understand it's almost impossible to care for someone with Alzheimer's, for example, in your home. However, there is much more to caring for people than just meeting their physical needs. We all have emotional and companionship needs, and it's not enough to place someone off in a home and say, "I've done my part."

I could tell you heartbreaking stories of people locked away in nursing homes who haven't seen or heard from their family members in years. I could tell you about church members who lashed out at me when I first went to visit them, because they had given their lives to the church and nobody from the church had visited them in years. They felt used, abused, and forgotten. They had a right to be angry and upset. This is why Paul says that when we fail to provide for our loved ones, we are denying the faith and are worse than unbelievers, because people who have never even known the love of Christ know how to comfort and care for their loved ones.

The caring and comfort of loved ones are behaviors I've observed and cherished about my numerous trips to South Korea. In the Asian culture, the elderly are treated with dignity, respect, and honor. We can learn many valuable lessons by imitating their behavior. As Christians, we are held to an even higher standard, because we have experienced the love of Christ firsthand in our lives. We are challenged to let the love of Christ flow through our lives to everyone we meet, but especially to our families. We put our faith into practice as we care for the elderly, especially our parents and grandparents. It is a sign of godliness.

Respecting the elderly is also repayment for earlier care. Mothers will often remind their children of all they have gone through for them, when they are trying to get the children to do something for them. I've heard a number of comedians quote their mothers as saying, "I brought you into this world and I can take you out!" Mothers sometimes have ways of reminding us of all the sacrifices they have made on our behalf. But that's okay, because we so easily forget all of the hard work and effort that went into raising us to adulthood. The Bible says that by showing love and respect to our parents, we are, in a sense, repaying them for all of their arduous work, dedication, and sacrifice. It's the least we can do for all they have done for us! Look again at verse 4. *The Message* paraphrase is even clearer. It reads,

> If a widow has family members to take care of her, let
> them learn that religion begins at their own doorstep

and that they should pay back with gratitude some of what they have received. This pleases God immensely. (1Timothy 5:4, *The Message*).

Some of the harshest words Jesus ever uttered were directed toward religious leaders who refused to care for their parents. In Matthew 15, the Pharisees had just sanctimoniously asked Jesus why His disciples didn't ceremonially wash their hands before they ate. Jesus turned to them and said,

> And why do you break the commandment of God for the sake of your tradition? For God commanded, "Honor your father and your mother," and, "Whoever reviles father or mother must surely die." But you say, "If anyone tells his father or his mother, 'What you would have gained from me is given to God,' he need not honor his father." So for the sake of your tradition, you have made void the word of God. You hypocrites! Well, did Isaiah prophesy of you, when he said: "This people honors me with their lips, but their heart is far from me; in vain do they worship me, teaching as doctrines the commandments of men" (Matthew 15:3–9).

Apparently, the Pharisees were withholding money from their parents and claiming they were giving it to God. But Jesus charged that in so doing, they were nullifying the word of God, because they should have been using the money to take care of their parents. This was an especially acute problem in Jesus's day, because there was no Social Security, no Medicaid, no drug plan … nothing! The elderly were completely at the mercy of their children, especially the widows. This is again why Paul declares in 1 Timothy 5:5, "She who is truly a widow, left all alone, has set her hope on God and continues in supplications and prayers night and day."

The widow had nowhere else to turn; if her children did not fulfill their responsibility, she was destined for a life of poverty and heartache. It reminds me of the poor, elderly widows I've often encountered on the streets in Russia. They are out in the streets begging, often in the bitter cold, because they have nowhere else to turn. Ironically, those religious leaders who thought they were so godly, were missing out on a key opportunity to put their faith into practice by not taking care of their loved ones. This is why Jesus said, "They honor me with their lips, but their hearts are far from me." Our actions speak much louder than our words.

When you really stop and think about it, do you believe we can ever fully repay our parents for all they have done for us? Most parents will agree it's a lot tougher being a parent than they thought it would be back before they got the job. The least we can do is honor and respect our parents. With this in mind, I want to challenge you with an assignment. This is something practical you can do to put your faith into action. If your parents are still living, I want to encourage you to write a letter and thank them for all that they have done for you. I heard about a man who did this, and his parents actually framed the letter and hung it in their living room! All it will cost you is a little bit of time and the price of a stamp, but it just might become one of your parents' most prized possessions. An attitude of gratitude is essential to living a godly life.

So, let me ask you a question: Would you like to be involved in an activity that pleases God immensely? The Bible clearly says respecting our elders is pleasing in God's sight. We all want God's smile of approval. We all want our lives to find favor with Him. God's word says one of the surefire ways of doing this is by loving, honoring, and respecting the elderly. Look a final time at 1 Timothy 5:4. Again, it says, "But if a widow has children or grandchildren, let them first learn to show godliness to their own household and to make some return to their parents, for this is pleasing in the sight of God."

Let's focus on this final phrase for just a moment. The Bible says this is pleasing in the sight of God! I don't know about you, but I have wonderful memories of times spent with my parents, grandparents, and even great-grandparents. This instruction to love and spend time with them is not a burden, but a joy! Alas, all of my grandparents are no longer living. I can't even begin to tell you how much influence they had on my life. I'm quite sure one of the reasons I'm in the ministry today is because of the prayers of my grandmother. I was deeply touched when she died and my aunt discovered my photograph taped to the inside cover of her Bible. It was a photo of me when I was a teenager. She had often told me she prayed for me every day. Apparently, this photograph was her visible reminder every morning to do that.

My prayer is that I can have this same type of godly influence on my children and future grandchildren … which brings me back around to the seniors reading this chapter. The Bible says there is a difference between the godly widows and the ungodly ones. Look carefully at how it makes this distinction beginning with verse 5: "She who is truly a widow, left all alone, has set her hope on God and continues in supplications and prayers night and day, but she who is self-indulgent is dead even while she lives" (1 Timothy 5:5–6).

The godly widows demonstrate a daily dependence upon God, but the ungodly widows are self-indulgent. Some translations declare, "only interested in pleasure." It also states, "They are dead even while they live." This passage is a wakeup call to all seniors who want to drop out of the Lord's work once they retire. God isn't finished with you yet! God wants you to finish just as strongly as you started. Let me remind you of the story of a man who finished well. His adventures are recorded in the book of Joshua, chapter 14. Look at what the text says, beginning with verse 6:

> Then the people of Judah came to Joshua at Gilgal. And Caleb the son of Jephunneh the Kenizzite said to him, "You know what the Lord said to Moses the man of God in Kadesh-barnea concerning you and

me. I was forty years old when Moses the servant of the Lord sent me from Kadesh-barnea to spy out the land, and I brought him word again as it was in my heart. But my brothers who went up with me made the heart of the people melt; yet I wholly followed the Lord my God. And Moses swore on that day, saying, 'Surely the land on which your foot has trodden shall be an inheritance for you and your children forever, because you have wholly followed the Lord my God.' And now, behold, the Lord has kept me alive, just as he said, these forty-five years since the time that the Lord spoke this word to Moses, while Israel walked in the wilderness. And now, behold, I am this day eighty-five years old. I am still as strong today as I was in the day that Moses sent me; my strength now is as my strength was then, for war and for going and coming. So now give me this hill country of which the Lord spoke on that day, for you heard on that day how the Anakim were there, with great fortified cities. It may be that the Lord will be with me, and I shall drive them out just as the Lord said." Then Joshua blessed him, and he gave Hebron to Caleb the son of Jephunneh for an inheritance. Therefore Hebron became the inheritance of Caleb the son of Jephunneh the Kenizzite to this day, because he wholly followed the Lord, the God of Israel (Joshua 14:6–14).

"So, why was Caleb blessed?" you ask. Caleb was blessed because he followed the Lord wholeheartedly all the days of his life! He did not slack off. He did not back down. He gave God his best all the days of his life. So, what about you? Are you following the Lord wholeheartedly? Are you giving Him your best? I certainly hope so, because the Lord deserves our best all the days of our lives. It is our responsibility to live this way, and it is our children's responsibility to respect the elders whom God has placed in their lives. This idea leads directly into our next chapter, where we will discover we are never too old to serve the Lord.

CHAPTER THREE

~~~~~~~~~~~~~~~~~~~~~~~~~~~~~~~~~~~~~~~

You're Never Too Old

The year was AD 155, and the persecution was intense. It had swept across the Roman Empire and had come to the city of Smyrna. The proconsul of Smyrna put out an order that Polycarp, the bishop of Smyrna, be found, arrested, and brought to the public arena for execution because of his faith in Christ. They found Polycarp and brought him before thousands of spectators screaming for blood. However, when the proconsul saw him, he had compassion on this man, who was almost one hundred years old. He signaled for the crowd to be quiet, and to Polycarp he said, "Curse the Christ and live."

The crowd waited in eager anticipation for this old man to answer. In an amazingly strong voice, he said, "Eighty and six years have I served him, and he has done me no wrong. How could I curse my King who saved me?" The judge then threatened to burn him alive. To this, Polycarp said that the fire would last for only a moment, in contrast to the eternal flame in his heart, which would never go out. Finally, he was tied to a post in the middle of the pyre, and just before he was consumed by the flames, he looked to heaven and prayed in a loud voice, "Lord God, I thank you that you have deemed me worthy of this moment, so that, jointly with your martyrs, I may share in the cup of Christ … for this … I bless and glorify you. Amen."

Where did Polycarp find the courage to stand firm in the middle of such a desperate situation? I believe in his testimony we detect his character. This man was totally committed to the Lord Jesus Christ. He understood where his strength came from, and after eighty-six years of service, he was not about to deny his convictions. He understood the truth that I want to try to communicate in this chapter, which is, you're never too old to serve the Lord! You're never too old to be used by God. You're never too old to faithfully follow the Lord Jesus Christ. In order to help us comprehend this, I want to highlight a number of saints who were used by God at a ripe old age.

Noah

In Genesis 6, we read about Noah finding favor in the eyes of the Lord. Incredibly, he found favor in the eyes of the Lord during a time when the world had gone mad. The Bible says the world was filled with wickedness, corruption, and evil. Things were so bad that God regretted creating the world and made the decision to destroy it. However, Noah found favor with God, and God instructed Noah to build an ark to save himself and his family members, along with two of every kind of bird and other animal. Noah was five hundred years old when the Lord spoke to him. He worked on the ark for one hundred years, before God enclosed Noah, his family, and all of the animals in the ark. Genesis 7:6 simply records, "Noah was six hundred years old when the flood of waters came upon the earth."

The floods came. The earth and most of its inhabitants were destroyed. Noah and his family survived, because a five-hundred-year-old man had found favor in the eyes of God! Obviously, no one lives this long in our world today, but God established early-on his desire to use people who are fully committed to Him despite their age. Noah is our first biblical example of age not being the determining factor when it comes to being used by God.

Abraham

In Genesis 18, angels visit Abraham in his old age and tell him he is going to have a son. Sarah, his elderly wife, is listening in on the conversation, and she laughs when she hears this news, since she is well past the childbearing years. Later, when the angel confronts her about laughing, she denies it. Ironically, the son is named Isaac, which means, "One who laughs." But to really understand this story, we have to go all the way back to Genesis 12, where God originally established His covenant with Abraham. The Bible says,

> The LORD had said to Abram, "Leave your country, your people and your father's household and go to the land I will show you. I will make you into a great nation and I will bless you; I will make your name great, and you will be a blessing. I will bless those who bless you, and whoever curses you I will curse; and all peoples on earth will be blessed through you." So Abram left, as the LORD had told him; and Lot went with him. Abram was seventy-five years old when he set out from Haran. He took his wife Sarai, his nephew Lot, all the possessions they had accumulated and the people they had acquired in Haran, and they set out for the land of Canaan, and they arrived there. (Genesis 12:1–5).

Did you happen to notice how old Abraham was when God called him into service? He was seventy-five years old! Have you ever stopped to think that your greatest accomplishments for the Lord might still be in your future? So many of us, of all ages, want to look back and admire our past performances, but Jesus says, "Look unto the fields that are white already unto harvest!" There is so much work to be done that we must continue to press on.

God made a covenant with Abraham, and to his credit, at age seventy-five, he obeyed. He packed up his family and all of his belongings, followed the promptings from the Lord, and moved. He did this despite lots of trouble and difficulty. It would have been much easier to have kicked back and relaxed at age seventy-five. He had problems with his nephew. They eventually separated. Later, following a series of Lot's bad decisions, Abraham had to go and rescue him.

Abraham was not getting any younger. He moved his family fifteen hundred miles on foot and by camel! This was a long time before North American Van Lines! He actually moved to a new country. He had struggles with the people in this new land, as well as problems in his own family. And, I imagine, he was beginning to wonder if it really was God's voice he had heard back in Haran. But listen to these reassuring words from the Lord in Genesis 15, where God renews His covenant with Abraham:

> After this, the word of the LORD came to Abram in a vision: "Do not be afraid, Abram. I am your shield, your very great reward." But Abram said, "O Sovereign LORD, what can you give me since I remain childless and the one who will inherit my estate is Eliezer of Damascus?" And Abram said, "You have given me no children; so a servant in my household will be my heir." Then the word of the LORD came to him: "This man will not be your heir, but a son coming from your own body will be your heir." He took him outside and said, "Look up at the heavens and count the stars—if indeed you can count them." Then he said to him, "So shall your offspring be." Abram believed the

LORD, and he credited it to him as righteousness (Genesis 15:1–6).

Again, to his credit, Abraham believed. God said it. Abraham believed it. This settled the issue in his heart, but in chapter 16, Abraham and Sarah tried to do what so many of us try to do. They decided, since they were not getting any younger, they would help God hurry the plan along. Sarah told Abraham to sleep with her handmaiden. This was a common practice in those days, and the child produced from the union would have been known as Abraham's son. This is what happened, and Ishmael was born; but this still did not solve the problem, because jealousy arose between Sarah and Hagar.

By the way, this all happened when Abraham was eighty-six years old! Can you imagine having to deal with all of this at the age of eighty-six? I can't even imagine having a baby in the house at that age! But God's timing is not our timing. It was thirteen years later, when Abraham was ninety-nine years old, that God came again to confirm the covenant. Abraham was seventy-five when God first spoke to him. He had been waiting for twenty-four years for God to fulfill His promise! Think about it—twenty-four years! And we get upset when God doesn't immediately answer the prayer we prayed last week. It's no wonder Abraham is held up as an example of faith. He was not getting any younger and the promised child still had not arrived, but notice what happened in chapter 17:

> When Abram was ninety-nine years old, the LORD appeared to him and said, "I am God Almighty; walk before me and be blameless. I will confirm my covenant between me and you and will greatly increase your numbers" (Genesis 17:1–2).

Now, drop down to verse 15.

God also said to Abraham, "As for Sarai your wife, you are no longer to call her Sarai; her name will be Sarah. I will bless her and will surely give you a son by her. I will bless her so that she will be the mother of nations; kings of peoples will come from her." Abraham fell facedown; he laughed and said to himself, "Will a son be born to a man a hundred years old? Will Sarah bear a child at the age of ninety?" (Genesis 17:15–17).

Now, please look very carefully at verse 19.

Then God said, "Yes, but your wife Sarah will bear you a son, and you will call him Isaac. I will establish my covenant with him as an everlasting covenant for his descendants after him" (Genesis 17:19).

So, God renewed His covenant with Abraham; then finally in Chapter 18, three visitors came to confirm in person what Abraham had been told in his vision from God. Abraham and Sarah both laughed when they heard this news, but this was not a scoffing laugh or a laugh of unbelief. It was the laughter of joy at what God was going to do. Certainly Sarah had questions, as was indicated by her response in verse 12, when she says, "After I am worn out and my master is old, will I now have this pleasure?" (Genesis 18:12).

There was joy in Abraham's house, because they knew, with confidence, that the angel was exactly right when he said in verse 14, "Is anything too hard for the LORD?" (Genesis 18:14) Nothing is too difficult for God! Is anything too difficult for the Lord? Obviously, the answer is, "No!" We see evidence of this in Chapter 21, when Sarah gives birth to Isaac at ninety years old, and Abraham is one hundred! So Abraham believed the impossible, and God credited it to him as righteousness.

Now, what does this have to do with those of us who are aging? In an effort to answer this question, let me draw your attention to Romans 4:18–25, where God's word says,

> Against all hope, Abraham in hope believed and so became the father of many nations, just as it had been said to him, "So shall your offspring be." Without weakening in his faith, he faced the fact that his body was as good as dead—since he was about a hundred years old—and that Sarah's womb was also dead. Yet he did not waver through unbelief regarding the promise of God, but was strengthened in his faith and gave glory to God, being fully persuaded that God had power to do what he had promised. This is why "it was credited to him as righteousness." The words "it was credited to him" were written not for him alone, but also for us, to whom God will credit righteousness—for us who believe in him who raised Jesus our Lord from the dead. He was delivered over to death for our sins and was raised to life for our justification (Romans 4:18–25).

The Bible says, "Against all hope—he believed!" When he was as good as dead—he believed! When things seemed impossible—he believed! Let me challenge you with the words of the angel: "Is anything too difficult for the Lord?" Abraham believed, and God credited it to him as righteousness. God demonstrated His faithfulness over and over again in Abraham's life, just like He has demonstrated himself over and over again in our lives! Our lives are a testimony that nothing is too difficult for God! As Polycarp testified, "For many years I have served him and he has done me no wrong." Nothing is too challenging for God! If God can give a child to a one-hundred-year-old man and his ninety-year-old wife, then

He can take care of whatever you are going through. You're never too old to serve the Lord. He wants to use you at any age.

Caleb

In the previous chapter, I touched on the fact that Caleb was eighty-five years old when he set out to claim his portion of the Promised Land! He said to Joshua,

> And now, behold, I am this day eighty-five years old. I am still as strong today as I was in the day that Moses sent me; my strength now is as my strength was then, for war and for going and coming. So now give me this hill country of which the Lord spoke on that day, for you heard on that day how the Anakim were there, with great fortified cities. It may be that the Lord will be with me, and I shall drive them out just as the Lord said (Joshua 14:10b–12).

Caleb was just as anxious to serve the Lord at eighty-five as he had been at forty. Age should not curb our enthusiasm for the Lord's work. He was ready to get busy. He had been ready for forty-five years! Look at how the passage ends, starting with verse 13:

> Then Joshua blessed Caleb son of Jephunneh and gave him Hebron as his inheritance. So Hebron has belonged to Caleb son of Jephunneh the Kenizzite ever since, because he followed the LORD, the God of Israel, wholeheartedly. (Hebron used to be called Kiriath Arba after Arba, who was the greatest man among the Anakites.) Then the land had rest from war (Joshua 14:13–15).

Caleb led the charge to take the Promised Land. Do you remember what the spies were afraid of back at Kadesh Barnea, when they first brought back the negative report? They said, "The Anakites were there and we appeared as grasshoppers in their sight." Did you notice whom the city was named after, before Caleb arrived at eighty-five years old? It was named after Arba, the greatest man among the Anakites, but this didn't matter to Caleb. He said, "I want that city and I'm going to take it!" Do you think there might have still been some Anakites there? Well, of course, they were still there, but Caleb went straight up and defeated them. He set the example for all of the other tribes. He was the first one to take his inheritance in the Promised Land, at the ripe old age of eighty-five. You are never too old to serve the Lord!

Daniel

Daniel was a young man when he was carted off to Babylon. He was only a youth when he and his friends found favor in the eyes of King Nebuchadnezzar. However, many years have passed by the time we reach chapter 6 and discover Daniel's friendship with King Darius. Cyrus and his troops captured the city and killed most of the officials, although Daniel was spared, and Cyrus's uncle, Darius the Mede, became the new leader at the age of sixty-two. Darius apparently took a liking to Daniel, because we are told that Daniel was appointed as one of three administrators over the kingdom. He did his job so well that Darius was making plans to appoint him as the leader over the entire kingdom. Look at what the text says at the beginning of chapter 6:

> It pleased Darius to appoint 120 satraps to rule
> throughout the kingdom, with three administrators
> over them, one of whom was Daniel. The satraps
> were made accountable to them so that the king

might not suffer loss. Now Daniel so distinguished
himself among the administrators and the satraps
by his exceptional qualities that the king planned
to set him over the whole kingdom (Daniel 6:1–3).

Of course, jealousy is an ugly trait, and the other leaders were
envious and jealous of Daniel's talent and ability. They were so
envious and jealous they sought to find a way to destroy Daniel.
However, the reputation of Daniel made their task very difficult.
Look at the text beginning in verse 4:

At this, the administrators and the satraps tried
to find grounds for charges against Daniel in his
conduct of government affairs, but they were unable
to do so. They could find no corruption in him,
because he was trustworthy and neither corrupt nor
negligent. Finally these men said, "We will never
find any basis for charges against this man Daniel
unless it has something to do with the law of his
God" (Daniel 6:4–5).

I love these verses, because of what we read between the lines.
You've got all of these people who are envious and jealous of Daniel.
They are seeking to destroy him, but they can't find anything to
charge him with, because his character is so impeccable. They
tried to find something wrong with his work, with his handling
of government affairs, but they could find nothing. The text says,
"They could find no corruption in him," but it doesn't stop there. It
goes on to say, "They could find no corruption in him, because he
was trustworthy and neither corrupt nor negligent." In other words,
Daniel did his job well. He did his work with integrity, skill, and
wisdom. He did his job so well that even his enemies couldn't find
anything bad to say about him. Finally, they came to the conclusion
recorded in verse 5, which says, "We will never find any basis for

charges against this man Daniel unless it has something to do with the law of his God" (Daniel 6:5).

What were they really saying? They were really saying that Daniel was a man of such integrity and faithfulness to his religion that the only way they could bring a charge against him was for them to come up with something that went against his faith. And, of course, this was exactly what they did. But before we get to that, let's stay here for just one moment longer. Someone once said, "A good reputation is more valuable than money." The Bible says an overseer is to have a good reputation with outsiders. And the writer of Proverbs reminds us, "The man of integrity walks securely, but he who takes crooked paths will be found out" (Proverbs 10:9).

Daniel had an excellent reputation. He walked in integrity. Now let's see what happened next. Look at the text beginning with verse 6:

> So the administrators and the satraps went as a group to the king and said: "O King Darius, live forever! The royal administrators, prefects, satraps, advisers and governors have all agreed that the king should issue an edict and enforce the decree that anyone who prays to any god or man during the next thirty days, except to you, O king, shall be thrown into the lions' den. Now, O king, issue the decree and put it in writing so that it cannot be altered—in accordance with the laws of the Medes and Persians, which cannot be repealed." So, King Darius put the decree in writing (Daniel 6:6–9).

They basically appealed to King Darius's ego by getting him to issue a decree saying everyone must pray to him alone during the next thirty days. If they did not, then they would be thrown into the lions' den. They tricked him. They lied to him. They said everyone had agreed to it, but obviously, Daniel had not agreed. At any rate, the king was deceived. He made the decree and put it in writing—which is important, because, in those days, once it was put into writing, it could not be changed, even by the king. Now look at verse 10:

> Now when Daniel learned that the decree had been published, he went home to his upstairs room where the windows opened toward Jerusalem. Three times a day he got down on his knees and prayed, giving thanks to his God, just as he had done before(Daniel 6:10).

I love this verse because it shows the faithfulness, courage, and consistency of Daniel. Daniel knew exactly what he was doing. The verse begins by saying, "Now when Daniel learned that the decree had been published." I'm sure he could see the treachery behind it. I'm sure he was close enough to the king to realize that the king had been duped, but Daniel didn't change anything about what he had been doing. He went to his room, opened his windows toward Jerusalem, got down on his knees, and prayed, giving thanks to God, just like he had done before. He wasn't going to be intimidated; but even more importantly, he wasn't going to bow down and pray to anyone other than His Father in heaven. He was a profile in courage, faithfulness, and consistency. The Bible also says he went to his room and did this three times a day!

I think you know the rest of the story. They came and discovered Daniel praying. They went back to the king and asked him if he hadn't issued a decree about praying to other gods. He said that he had, and then they told him they had caught Daniel praying to another God. The king realized he had been duped, and he tried frantically to save Daniel until sundown, but the folks insisted he follow through with his order and have Daniel thrown into the lions' den. He issued the order to be carried out, but before Daniel was thrown in, the king said to him in verse 16, "May your God, whom you serve continually, rescue you!" (Daniel 10:16)

The king stayed up all night worrying. He couldn't sleep, and he wouldn't eat. Let's pick up the story at verse 19:

> At the first light of dawn, the king got up and hurried to the lions' den. When he came near the den, he called to Daniel in an anguished voice, "Daniel, servant of the living God, has your God, whom you serve continually, been able to rescue you from the lions?" Daniel answered, "O king, live forever! My God sent his angel, and he shut the mouths of the lions. They have not hurt me, because I was found innocent in his sight. Nor have I ever done any wrong before you, O king." The king was overjoyed and gave orders to lift Daniel out of the den. And when Daniel was lifted from the den, no wound was found on him, because he had trusted in his God (Daniel 10:19–23).

God sent His angel and delivered Daniel from the lions' den. He was delivered, the Bible says, because he had trusted in his God and he was innocent in His sight. Now, before you think, "Well, the lions were just not hungry that night," look at verse 24:

> At the king's command, the men who had falsely accused Daniel were brought in and thrown into the lions' den, along with their wives and children. And before they reached the floor of the den, the lions overpowered them and crushed all their bones (Daniel 10:24).

Oh, yeah, they were hungry, but God protected and spared Daniel because of his faithfulness. The king was so impressed with what God had done for Daniel that he issued the following decree:

I issue a decree that in every part of my kingdom people must fear and reverence the God of Daniel. For he is the living God and he endures forever; his kingdom will not be destroyed, his dominion will never end. He rescues and he saves; he performs signs and wonders in the heavens and on the earth. He has rescued Daniel from the power of the lions (Daniel 10:26–27).

The chapter then closes by saying Daniel prospered during the reigns of Darius and Cyrus. So what can we learn from the story of Daniel and the lions' den? We can learn that God honors a lifetime of faithful consistency. Daniel's enemies knew he was so committed to his daily prayers that they decided to use his devotion against him. They got the king to issue a ludicrous decree, and Daniel knew all about the decree. He knew the danger. He understood the risk, but nothing was going to come between Daniel and his daily time with the Lord.

A life of faithful consistency over time will produce spiritual results. We clearly see this in the life of Daniel. He set a godly example that we should all want to follow. It started when he was taken into captivity as a teenager and was chosen to receive special training to serve in the king's court. It continued throughout his lifetime as he served a variety of pagan kings and challenged each of them to live up to godly standards. And it stayed with him into his old age. Scholars estimate the events recorded in chapters 5 and 6 occurred when Daniel was at least eighty years old. Consistency over time equals maturity. I pray God will help us to follow the example of Daniel, because his life illustrates our theme—you are never too old to serve the Lord. But this theme is not limited to the Old Testament.

Zechariah and Elizabeth

Zechariah and Elizabeth were well up in years when the angel appeared to Zechariah and told him his wife Elizabeth was going to have a baby. The story begins in Luke 1, beginning with verse 5. It says,

> In the days of Herod, king of Judea, there was a priest named Zechariah, of the division of Abijah. And he had a wife from the daughters of Aaron, and her name was Elizabeth. And they were both righteous before God, walking blamelessly in all the commandments and statutes of the Lord. But they had no child, because Elizabeth was barren, and both were advanced in years (Luke 1:5–7).

Names are significant in the Bible. Zechariah means, "The Lord remembers," and Elizabeth means, "My God is faithful." They were both of priestly descent from the line of Aaron. The NIV Study Bible tells us that "from the time of David the priests were organized into twenty-four divisions, and Abijah was one of the heads of the priestly families."[7] Zechariah belonged to this division. Now, notice what the text says about both of them. It actually says four things about them:

1. "They were both righteous before God."
2. They both walked blamelessly in all the commandments and statutes of the Lord.
3. They were childless.
4. They were advanced in years.

Interestingly, the text says, "They were both righteous before God." In other words, they both loved the Lord. They both sought

---

[7] Kenneth Barker, General Editor, The NIV Study Bible (Grand Rapids: Zondervan Bible Publishers, 1985), p. 1535.

to do what was right. They both were obedient, keeping all the commandments and laws of the Lord. We know this was true because the text goes on to say, They both walked "blamelessly in all the commandments and statutes of the Lord."

This doesn't mean they were sinless, but it does mean they were both faithful and sincere when it came to obeying the Lord's commands. They were each blessed with a godly spouse. You are a blessed person if you have a godly mate, and you should be thankful for him or her. So, with all of this being the case, don't you find it ironic that they were childless? In our world today, many choose to remain childless. I also understand the inability to have children is not seen or understood to be a sign of disapproval from God in our world today. We realize there are many medical reasons why couples are unable to bear children.

However, in the first century, the inability to have children was seen as a judgment from God. In their culture, this meant something must be wrong or that God was upset with them for some reason. Therefore, the fact that they were both living upright and blameless lives before God, and yet were unable to have children, must have been very difficult for them to comprehend. We will read in just a moment where the angel says to Zechariah, "God has answered your prayer." So, obviously this was something Zechariah prayed about often, even though they were now advanced in years. The Bible doesn't say exactly how old they were, but the insinuation is that Elizabeth is already well beyond the age for childbearing … but of course, nothing is impossible with God.

We seem to have the idea that if we are living right, if we are being obedient to God, and if we are submitting our lives to Him, then God is obligated to do what we want. But here we find a couple who remained faithful to God well into their twilight years, even though things had not gone their way. I know someone is going to say, "But God does answer their prayer, and things did turn out well for them." This is true, but I will submit to you that I believe they would have continued to live for the Lord even if things had not turned around. They were already well advanced in years. So, obviously, they had already lived a long time with this "shame" hanging over their heads. Yet the Bible describes them as righteous and blameless. They modeled consistency and faithfulness despite their circumstances, and, for that alone, I believe they should be applauded. But notice what happens next. Let's pick up with verse 8: "Now while he was serving as priest before God when his division was on duty, according to the custom of the priesthood, he was chosen by lot to enter the temple of the Lord and burn incense" (Luke 1:8–9).

This was a very rare and special duty. One of my commentaries says,

> There were twenty-four divisions of priests in Israel at this time ... each division took a turn yearly to serve for a week. Only one priest at a time had the honor of burning the incense at the altar ... there were so many priests that this special honor might just come once in a lifetime, or perhaps not at all.[8]

This was a once-in-a-lifetime experience for Zechariah. I'm sure he was very excited about it. He might have even seen this as confirmation of God's smile of approval upon his life, after all those years of faithfulness. I'm sure he was happy about this holy privilege. I'm confident he prepared himself to the best of his ability, but he wasn't prepared for what happened next. Look at the text. It says,

> And the whole multitude of the people were praying outside at the hour of incense. And there appeared to him an angel of the Lord standing on the right side of the altar of incense. And Zechariah was

---

[8] Bruce Larson, *The Preacher's Commentary Series*, Vol. 26, *Luke*, Edited by Lloyd J. Ogilvie (Nashville, Thomas Nelson, 1983), p. 26–27.

troubled when he saw him, and fear fell upon him
(Luke 1:10–12).

Imagine you have been waiting all of your life to step inside this
holy place. You draw back the curtain and step inside, and once your
eyes adjust to the dim lighting, you see an angel of the Lord standing
beside the altar of incense. I don't care what you say, you also would
be frightened! The Bible says he was troubled and fear fell upon him.
He probably wanted to turn around and run, but before he could flee
the angel spoke to him and said, "Do not be afraid, Zechariah, for
your prayer has been heard, and your wife Elizabeth will bear you a
son, and you shall call his name John" (Luke 1:13).

The angel told him not to be afraid. He called him by name. He
said, "[Y]our prayer has been heard, and your wife Elizabeth will
bear you a son, and you shall call his name John." So he began by
telling him not to be afraid, but how can you not be afraid when an
angel appears in front of you and calls you by name? But even more
remarkable, he declared, "[Y]our prayer has been heard." Obviously,
Zechariah had been praying for a son, because the angel said that his
wife, Elizabeth, would bear a son in answer to his prayers. Finally,
he said in this verse, "[A]nd you shall call his name John." The
name John means, "gift of God." So, after all those years of living
righteous lives, all those years of walking blamelessly by keeping
God's commands and statutes, God was answering their prayers and
giving them a son. But this was not going to be just any son; look at
how the passage continues:

> And you will have joy and gladness, and many will
> rejoice at his birth, for he will be great before the
> Lord. And he must not drink wine or strong drink,
> and he will be filled with the Holy Spirit, even from
> his mother's womb. And he will turn many of the
> children of Israel to the Lord their God, and he
> will go before him in the spirit and power of Elijah,

to turn the hearts of the fathers to the children, and the disobedient to the wisdom of the just, to make ready for the Lord a people prepared (Luke 1:14–17).

This child was set apart to be special from birth. The angel said he would bring joy and gladness into Zechariah's heart and many would rejoice at his birth. He would be a great man of God. Of course, we know this prophecy was fulfilled. Jesus once said of John the Baptist, "I tell you, among those born of women none is greater than John. Yet the one who is least in the kingdom of God is greater than he" (Luke 7:28).

He was not to drink alcohol, and he would be filled with the Holy Spirit from birth! He would walk in the spirit of Elijah and cause many to turn to the Lord, with fathers loving and caring for their children and the disobedient embracing wisdom, preparing the way for the Lord. This was going to be a very special child.

Obviously, you would think Zechariah would be overcome with joy. This was the answer to his beseeching prayer. This was even better than anything he could have hoped for or imagined. He was not only having a son, but this son was going to be the forerunner to the Messiah. He was going to be a great prophet and preacher, turning the hearts of many back to God. What more could a priest want? But instead of rejoicing, he asked a question that is filled with doubt and even shows lack of faith. He said, "How shall I know this? For I am an old man, and my wife is advanced in years" (Luke 1:18).

I don't want to be too hard on Zechariah. We know he was frightened. He was probably doing well just to stay on his feet. What would you do if an angel appeared to you and called you by name? But this was absolutely the wrong way to respond. However, I'm actually a little encouraged by this development. The Bible has already called him an upright and blameless man, and even he said the wrong thing. This gives all of us hope, but notice how the angel responded. He quickly set Zechariah straight. He boomed, "I am

Gabriel. I stand in the presence of God, and I was sent to speak to you and to bring you this good news" (Luke 1:19).

In other words, you don't know who you are talking to, Zechariah. How dare you question anything I have to say? These words came straight from the throne room of heaven; therefore, you are going to have to suffer consequences for your doubt and lack of faith. Look at verse 20: "And behold, you will be silent and unable to speak until the day that these things take place, because you did not believe my words, which will be fulfilled in their time" (Luke 1:20).

Have you ever thought about what a horrible punishment this was for a priest? I can't think of much worse that could have been done to him. He had just seen an angel from the very presence of God, and he couldn't tell anyone about it. Priests, pastors, religious leaders—we make our living by talking. But now he was banished to months of silence, because of his unbelief. It was the most incredible experience of his life, and he was unable to tell anyone about it.

Can you imagine how frustrating this must have been for him? Can you understand how upset he must have been with himself? I'm sure for many silent months, he replayed this conversation over and over in his mind, and each time he incredulously said to himself, "How dumb are you? You were talking with an angel sent from God, and you doubted what he said." It's especially tough to be a communicator, and then not have the ability to communicate, but he tried. Look at verse 21:

> And the people were waiting for Zechariah, and they were wondering at his delay in the temple. And when he came out, he was unable to speak to them, and they realized that he had seen a vision in the temple. And he kept making signs to them and remained mute. And when his time of service was ended, he went to his home (Luke 1:21–23).

The people were starting to get worried. It didn't take this long to light incense. What was going on in there? When he came out, he couldn't talk, and they drew the logical conclusion: When a preacher can't talk, you know something is wrong! So he tried sign language, and they concluded that he had seen some type of vision. He must have been so upset with himself, because he couldn't even tell them about it. God heard my prayer. I'm going to have a son, but not just any son. He is going to be great! He couldn't tell them any of this, and when his time of service ended he went home. We then get a little glimpse into Elizabeth's thoughts in verses 24–25:

> After these days his wife Elizabeth conceived, and for five months she kept herself hidden, saying, "Thus the Lord has done for me in the days when he looked on me, to take away my reproach among people" (Luke 1:24–25).

This passage confirms what we said earlier about how their culture viewed barrenness. She was overjoyed, since God had looked upon her with favor and taken away her "reproach" among the people. Obviously, even though she was upright and blameless before the Lord, she understood her inability to have children as a reproach. She may or may not have felt this way personally, but she certainly understood that this was the way people felt toward her.

So the parents of John the Baptist were very unique and special people. They were righteous and blameless, but even righteous and blameless people can still make mistakes. Zechariah doubted the words of the angel, and Elizabeth allowed the reproach from the people to affect her relationship with God. Otherwise, she would not have been so overjoyed when she realized she was pregnant. This shows how good, godly people can sometimes make mistakes; therefore, we all need to rely upon the Lord every day and in all circumstances. Let's drop down to verse 57 and see how the story ends. It says,

> Now the time came for Elizabeth to give birth,
> and she bore a son. And her neighbors and relatives
> heard that the Lord had shown great mercy to her,
> and they rejoiced with her(Luke 1:57)

Just like the angel Gabriel had said to Zechariah earlier, there was great rejoicing when the baby was born. No doubt they were rejoicing because Elizabeth was able to give birth to a healthy baby boy, even though she was well advanced in years. They all considered this to be an act of great mercy from the Lord. They all rejoiced with her and, I'm sure, Zechariah also rejoiced, but he was still unable to speak. He probably thought by now this was a permanent condition, but let's continue …

> And on the eighth day they came to circumcise the
> child. And they would have called him Zechariah
> after his father, but his mother answered, "No; he
> shall be called John." And they said to her, "None of
> your relatives is called by this name." And they made
> signs to his father, inquiring what he wanted him
> to be called. And he asked for a writing tablet and
> wrote, "His name is John." And they all wondered
> (Luke 1:59–63).

On the eighth day, as was the Jewish custom, they took the boy to be circumcised, and this was also the time the name was officially given. Everyone assumed he would be named after his father, Zechariah, but when Elizabeth told them the child's name would be John, they couldn't believe it. The tradition was to at least name a child after someone in the family. So everyone was shocked that this devout couple was breaking away from tradition. Therefore, they turned to the father to settle this once and for all. He asked or signaled for a writing tablet and wrote, "His name is John," which you recall means, "gift of God." And the text says, "And they all wondered." But they had only a brief moment to be perplexed, because verse 64 records,

> And immediately his mouth was opened and his tongue loosed, and he spoke, blessing God. And fear came on all their neighbors. And all these things were talked about through all the hill country of Judea, and all who heard them laid them up in their hearts, saying, "What then will this child be?" For the hand of the Lord was with him (Luke 1:64–66).

We see that many supernatural events surrounded the birth of John the Baptist. It had been over four hundred years since a prophet had spoken in Israel. There had been no more prophets since the time of Malachi, but God was doing something significant with the birth of John the Baptist. He was to be the forerunner of Christ. Finally, Zechariah's tongue was loosed, and he was able to tell everyone about the encounter with the angel Gabriel and what he had said about this boy. This caused the people to exclaim, "What then will this child be?" For it was very obvious that the hand of the Lord was with him, and it didn't take them long to find out the answer to their question, because the Bible goes on to say Zechariah was filled with the Holy Spirit and began to prophesy, pronouncing,

> Blessed be the Lord God of Israel, for he has visited and redeemed his people and has raised up a horn of salvation for us in the house of his servant David, as he spoke by the mouth of his holy prophets from of old, that we should be saved from our enemies and from the hand of all who hate us; to show the mercy promised to our fathers and to remember his holy covenant, the oath that he swore to our father Abraham, to grant us that we, being delivered from the hand of our enemies, might serve him without

fear, in holiness and righteousness before him all our days. And you, child, will be called the prophet of the Most High; for you will go before the Lord to prepare his ways, to give knowledge of salvation to his people in the forgiveness of their sins, because of the tender mercy of our God, whereby the sunrise shall visit us from on high to give light to those who sit in darkness and in the shadow of death, to guide our feet into the way of peace (Luke 1:68–79).

This passage is sometimes referred to as, "Zechariah's Song." In it he begins by praising God for sending a deliverer from the house and line of David. He would bring salvation and redeem his people. This entire section, of course, is talking about Jesus, but then he turns his attention to his son. He begins by disclosing that he will be called the prophet of the Most High. In Luke 7, Jesus reveals how John the Baptist fulfills this prophecy. He asks,

What did you go out into the wilderness to see? A reed shaken by the wind? What then did you go out to see? A man dressed in soft clothing? Behold, those who are dressed in splendid clothing and live in luxury are in kings' courts. What then did you go out to see? A prophet? Yes, I tell you, and more than a prophet. This is he of whom it is written, "Behold, I send my messenger before your face, who will prepare your way before you" (Luke 7:24–27).

Jesus is quoting directly from Malachi (Malachi 3:1), the last prophet to speak in the Old Testament, and he says John the Baptist is the fulfillment of this prophecy. He is the one to prepare the way for the Messiah. This folds right into the next statement made by Zechariah about his son, as he declares, "For you will go before the

Lord to prepare his ways." Of course, Jesus says the same thing about John in the passage we just read.

However, Zechariah goes on to say, "to give knowledge of salvation to his people in the forgiveness of their sins." All four gospels say John the Baptist came preaching a baptism of repentance for the forgiveness of sins. Finally, Zechariah concludes, "Because of the tender mercy of our God, whereby the sunrise shall visit us from on high, to give light to those who sit in darkness and in the shadow of death, to guide our feet into the way of peace." This means John ultimately came to point people to Christ. This passage is clearly talking about Jesus. He is the light of the world and the Prince of Peace. In fact, one of the greatest statements ever attributed to John the Baptist is where he cried, "He must increase, but I must decrease" (John 3:30).

John was a great prophet and preacher, but he clearly understood his role. He was taught well by his righteous and blameless parents to be obedient to the will of God. They illustrate our thesis—you are never too old to serve the Lord.

Simeon and Anna

Simeon and Anna are the next older godly saints to step out of the pages of scripture. Their story is found in Luke 2, beginning in verse 25:

> Now there was a man in Jerusalem, whose name was Simeon, and this man was righteous and devout, waiting for the consolation of Israel, and the Holy Spirit was upon him. And it had been revealed to him by the Holy Spirit that he would not see death before he had seen the Lord's Christ (Luke 2:25–26).

Can you imagine how Simeon must have felt when he saw the Christ child? The Bible says he was a righteous and devout man. It also says he was waiting for the consolation of Israel. Consolation comes from the Greek word *Paraklesis*, and it means, "comfort." So he was waiting on the comfort of Israel. This fits in well with many of the prophecies about the Messiah. For instance, Isaiah 40:1–3 imparts,

> Comfort, comfort my people, says your God. Speak tenderly to Jerusalem, and cry to her that her warfare is ended, that her iniquity is pardoned, that she has received from the Lord's hand double for all her sins. A voice cries: "In the wilderness prepare the way of the Lord; make straight in the desert a highway for our God."

Of course, others were waiting for this same comfort … such as Anna, whom we will meet in a few minutes. However, you might be wondering, How did he know it was the Messiah? It's a good question. How did he know this was the Messiah? The Bible simply says the Holy Spirit revealed it to him. Look again at verses 26 and 27:

> And it had been revealed to him by the Holy Spirit that he would not see death before he had seen the Lord's Christ. And he came in the Spirit into the temple, and when the parents brought in the child Jesus, to do for him according to the custom of the Law (Luke 2:26–27).

Simeon was a seasoned saint who walked by the Spirit. The Holy Spirit told him he would not die before he had the opportunity to see the Lord's Christ. He believed what God had told him, and then on a certain day, at a certain time, the Spirit nudged him to go to the temple. He was sensitive enough to the Spirit to sense and understand that God was telling him to go. So he went, and when he got there and saw the child with his parents, the Spirit confirmed to him, "That's the one." The Holy Spirit revealed to Simeon that Jesus was the Messiah. In other words, God kept his promise! He promised Simeon he would not die before he saw the Messiah, and here he was! Of course, Simeon was overcome with joy, and this devout man took the child into his arms and made a bold statement. Look at verses 28–30: "He took him up in his arms and blessed God and said, 'Lord, now you are letting your servant depart in peace, according to your word; for my eyes have seen your salvation'" (Luke 2:28–30).

Literally, Simeon is saying, "Now, you can release me. God, you are faithful. You have kept your promise. I have seen your deliverer." Jesus Christ is the ultimate fulfillment of God's plan. Simeon's praise signals the arrival of the Messiah. In reference to the Messiah, he says, "That you have prepared in the presence of all people" (Luke 2:31).

Upon first glance, you might think this verse simply means God did this in front of all of the people in the temple, or out in the open so everyone could see it, but the meaning of the word *prepared* goes much deeper. It means this action was not an afterthought on God's part. It was not plan B. God's plan was put into place before the foundation of the world. This is why the Bible says in 1 Peter 1:20, "He was foreknown before the foundation of the world but was made manifest in the last times for the sake of you." This is also why we read in Galatians 4:4–5,

> But when the fullness of time had come, God sent
> forth his Son, born of woman, born under the law,
> to redeem those who were under the law, so that we
> might receive adoption as sons.

God's plan from the very beginning of time was to send Jesus Christ as the Messiah to die in our place. It was also part of God's plan for Simeon to see the Messiah before he died. He proclaims Jesus to be, "A light for revelation to the Gentiles, and for glory to your people Israel" (Luke 2:32).

Notice whom Simeon says Jesus came to illumine. He came for the glory of your people Israel, but not for Israel alone. He also came, our text says, as a light for revelation to the Gentiles. This is very good news for us! Jesus came to save us! The good news of the gospel is for everyone to the very ends of the earth. Jesus Christ came to be a light for the nations! Look at Simeon's final prophecy in verses 34–35:

> And Simeon blessed them and said to Mary his mother, "Behold, this child is appointed for the fall and rising of many in Israel, and for a sign that is opposed (and a sword will pierce through your own soul also), so that thoughts from many hearts may be revealed" (Luke 2:34–35).

Simeon's prophecy reveals that many would accept and embrace the Messiah, while at the same time, many others would not. So, what about you? Will you receive and accept God's gift of love? Will you put your faith and trust in God's one and only Son? He really is the light of the world! He really did come to save us from our sins. However, we have another reason to believe. It is what I want to call the "confirmation." Look at the text beginning with verse 36:

> And there was a prophetess, Anna, the daughter of Phanuel, of the tribe of Asher. She was advanced in years, having lived with her husband seven years from when she was a virgin, and then as a widow until she was eighty-four. She did not depart from the temple, worshiping with fasting and prayer night and day. And coming up at that very hour she began to give thanks to God and to speak of

him to all who were waiting for the redemption of Jerusalem (Luke 2:36–38).

The Bible calls for two witnesses to confirm evidence and solidify the facts. Anna is our second witness. The Bible describes her as a godly widow who spent her days fasting and praying in the temple. The Bible also says she was eighty-four years old, which was well beyond the life expectancy of individuals during this period of time. However, at the very moment when Simeon was proclaiming the glory of this baby, she came forward and confirmed everything he had just said. The Bible says she began to give thanks and praise to God. She also began to speak of this child as the one they had been waiting for to redeem Jerusalem.

It's no coincidence that Simeon and Anna were both in the temple on this day. The combined testimonies of these two seasoned, faithful witnesses paint a portrait of a God who loves us so much He sent a Messiah, His one and only Son, named Jesus, to save us from our sins. God used both of them to bless and welcome His Son into the world. May we all someday be able to pray with Simeon, "Lord, now let your servant depart in peace …" He was able to depart in peace, because he understood God had kept His promises to him.

John the Apostle

The final elderly saint used mightily by God whom I want to examine in this chapter is the apostle John. Scholars debate, but most believe, that the gospel of John was written much later than the other three gospels. Matthew, Mark, and Luke are all dated before the fall of Jerusalem in AD 70. Mark's gospel is believed to be the first to have been written down, and it is often dated in the early fifties. In contrast, most scholars believe John was not written until much later—around AD 85.

If this is true, then most of the New Testament would have

already been completed before John added his portion with the gospel, then the three epistles, and finally the book of Revelation. We know John was exiled on the Isle of Patmos at a ripe old age, but we also know from the early church fathers that John was the pastor of the church in Ephesus for many years. So, near the end of his life, he was compelled to write his gospel, which emphasized the deity of Christ. He says near the end of the book,

> Now Jesus did many other signs in the presence of
> the disciples, which are not written in this book; but
> these are written so that you may believe that Jesus
> is the Christ, the Son of God, and that by believing
> you may have life in his name (John 20:30–31).

Ray Steadman begins his study of the gospel of John in *Adventuring through the Bible* by talking about how the gospel of John holds a special place in his heart, because it was written by the disciple who was the closest to Jesus. He basically says, "Sure, Matthew was a dedicated disciple, and Mark and Luke were committed followers, but most of Mark and Luke's information came from the testimony of others, but John is the beloved disciple." He is the one who leaned in close to Jesus at the Last Supper. He is the one who stood at the foot of the cross as Jesus died. He is the one whom Jesus entrusted with the care of his own mother. He even refers to himself as, "the disciple whom Jesus loved." He was part of Jesus's inner circle along with Peter and James. As such, he experienced several things the other disciples did not experience. He saw and heard more than any of the others, which is why this gospel is sometimes referred to as, "The Intimate Gospel." Pastor Steadman goes on to say, "John watched the life of Jesus more closely than any other person on earth—and John came away absolutely convinced of the deity of Christ."[9]

---

[9] Ray C. Stedman, *Adventuring through the Bible* (Grand Rapids: Discovery House Publishers, 1997), p. 528.

This is clearly the theme of the gospel of John—Jesus Christ is the Son of God. It was written by a man well advanced in years. He experienced the thrill of walking side by side with Jesus during his younger years. He lived long enough to see all of his fellow disciples martyred for their faith. He alone was left, and he gave us some of the richest words in the New Testament.

God wasn't finished with him, and He is not finished with you. This chapter illustrates that God is willing to use men and women to a ripe old age who are faithfully committed to Him. You are never too old to serve the Lord. We are challenged to remain faithful to Him all the days of our lives. Again, we are reminded of the words of Polycarp: "Eighty and six years have I served him, and he has done me no wrong. How could I curse my King who saved me?" The next chapter explores how we can remain faithful to the Lord on a daily basis.

CHAPTER FOUR

It's Better to Be Over the Hill than Under It!

It's Better to Be Over the Hill than Under It is the title of a book by Erma Bombeck. I believe she makes an excellent point. Life is for the living; therefore, we should make the most of each new day. I came across a quote that says, "The wisest are not the ones with the most years in their lives, but the ones with the most life in their years."[10]

How are you doing with putting life in your years? There is a beautiful lake near our home with a well-maintained walking path around it. It is perfect for those of us who enjoy taking a good, brisk stroll. However, the longer I've been walking the trail, the more I have noticed that it's the same people walking around the lake every day. Thousands live nearby, but only a few are taking advantage of this wonderful opportunity. I noticed the same phenomenon when we recently experienced a solar eclipse. I saw one neighbor step outside of his home to look at it!

Life was not meant to be lived vicariously through others on the television or through your smart device. Life was meant to be lived

---

[10] Max Lucado, _He Still Moves Stones_ (Dallas: Word Publishing, 1993), p. 76.

personally and experientially as you step out and enjoy the sunset, smell the flowers, and experience the eclipse. God has blessed us with the gifts of His creation. I stand in awe of His handiwork. I'm amazed by His creativity. I'm blessed by His attention to detail. Let me encourage you to put down your phone, turn off your television, shut down your computer, and step outside and experience Him in a new and fresh way. Put life into your years.

Oliver Wendell Holmes was once asked why he started studying Greek at the age of ninety-four. He replied, "Well, it's now or never."[11] J. C. Penney said, at the age of ninety-five, "My eyesight may be getting weaker, but my vision is increasing."[12] General Douglas MacArthur reportedly said, at the age of seventy-eight, "Nobody grows old by merely living a number of years. People grow old by deserting their ideals. Years may wrinkle the skin, but to give up interest wrinkles the soul."[13] Hugh Downs states, "The older you get, you find there's a tide that kind of goes out and leaves the rocks that are important."[14] Warren Wiersbe observes, "The older we get, the better we understand that life is brief and moves past very swiftly."[15] Psalm 90 is the only psalm attributed to Moses. He reminds us time is fleeting when he writes, "The years of our life are seventy, or even by reason of strength eighty; yet their span is but toil and trouble; they are soon gone, and we fly away" (Psalm 90:10).

Since this is true, let me make a few suggestions to help us get the most life out of our years. First, I would like to encourage you

---

[11] Ibid., p. 78.

[12] Ibid.

[13] Ibid., p.76–77.

[14] Hugh Downs, quoted in Philip L. Berman, *The Ageless Spirit: Reflections on Living Life to the Fullest in Midlife and the Years Beyond,* Edited by Connie Goldman (New York: Ballantine Books, 1992), p. 79.

[15] Warren W. Wiersbe, *The Wiersbe Bible Commentary: The Complete Old Testament (OT) in One Volume* / Edition 1 (Colorado Springs: David C. Cook, 2007), p. 973.

to number your days. Psalm 90:12 says, "So teach us to number our days that we may get a heart of wisdom" (Psalm 90:12).

The ancient Hebrews attributed the mind, will, and emotions to the heart. Moses clearly understood this. He faithfully led the children of Israel until he was 120 years old. In one of his last messages to the people, he said,

> See, I have set before you today life and good, death and evil. If you obey the commandments of the Lord your God that I command you today, by loving the Lord your God, by walking in his ways, and by keeping his commandments and his statutes and his rules, then you shall live and multiply, and the Lord your God will bless you in the land that you are entering to take possession of it. But if your heart turns away, and you will not hear, but are drawn away to worship other gods and serve them, I declare to you today, that you shall surely perish. You shall not live long in the land that you are going over the Jordan to enter and possess. I call heaven and earth to witness against you today, that I have set before you life and death, blessing and curse. Therefore choose life, that you and your offspring may live, loving the Lord your God, obeying his voice and holding fast to him, for he is your life and length of days (Deuteronomy 30:15–20a).

In this passage, Moses gives us the prescription for living a long, full life. If we desire to live the life God intends for us to live, then we must choose life. In other words, we must make the choice to live for the Lord, follow His commandments, obey His word, and follow His rules. This is the prescription for numbering your days. This doesn't mean to just consider the brevity of life; it means to consider how you are living your life on a daily basis. Again, it's more important to put life into your years than just to add more years to your life. Who cares how long you live if you are not really *living*? We all have this choice at every age, but as we age and the time window narrows, we begin to realize how important it is to make the most of the time we have remaining. As we watch the sands of time slip away in our hourglass, we realize the importance of living our lives according to God's standards. This is the point Paul was making to the widows in 1 Timothy when he wrote, "But she who is self-indulgent is dead even while she lives" (1 Timothy 5:6).

We don't want to fritter our lives away playing bingo, watching television, and gossiping on the telephone. We need to be involved in activities of significance. Of course, this doesn't mean we can't ever relax, but it does mean we want to live out our days in dignity by being involved in activities that further God's kingdom. So, the first suggestion for living your life to the fullest is to number your days.

The second suggestion is to find satisfaction in God. In fact, the secret to putting life into your years is found in verse 14 of Psalm 90. It declares, "Satisfy us in the morning with your steadfast love, that we may rejoice and be glad all our days" (Psalm 90:14).

My father was a bivocational pastor all of his adult life. This meant he often had to get up early and rush off to work to provide for his family. He found ways to have quiet times and personal devotions, but he had to squeeze them in where he could—on the run, in the midst of a hectic, fast-paced lifestyle. He told me once, after his retirement, how much he was enjoying having the time to read and study his Bible now that he did not have to get up and rush off to work first thing in the morning. He found satisfaction in the morning through his personal time with the Lord. This is actually what he was doing just before he died. He had just finished with his personal devotions when a heart attack took his life. He closed his eyes in death and opened them in heaven.

How are you doing with your personal times with the Lord? It's kind of like the humorous story of the couple who had been married for many years, and one afternoon they were driving along and got behind a car driven by a young, newlywed couple. In the first car, the wife was snuggling over close to her husband. The older lady said to her husband, "Oh, isn't that so sweet? Honey, do you remember when we used to do that? Why don't we do that anymore?"

The older man looked over at his wife and grunted, "Who moved?"

God is still there, just like he has always been. He wants us to grow in our relationship with Him. He is patiently waiting to spend quality time with you. Listen, no matter how long you have been a Christian, you can still grow in your Christian life, but we have to make quality time with Him a priority.

We are all pressed for time, but we make time for what is important to us. I came across a cartoon a few years ago that is one of my personal favorites. The cartoon depicts an exhausted-looking man with terribly bloodshot eyes from watching so much football on television, but the caption reads, "I wish I knew the Bible better!" We make time for what is important to us. Where does time with the Lord fit into your list of priorities? Psalm 5:3 says, "In the morning, O Lord, Thou wilt hear my voice; in the morning, I will order my prayer to thee and eagerly watch" (Psalm 5:3).

Please don't get hung up on when you have your time with God. You have to find a time that works best for you. Obviously, some people are morning people and others are night owls, but the point is that in order to grow, you have to find the time. We see this with all relationships. If you want a relationship to grow and develop, then there has to be an investment of time. Jesus modeled a life committed to time alone with God. For instance, Mark 1:35 tells us, "And in the early morning, while it was still dark, He arose and went out and departed to a lonely place, and was praying there."

If Jesus made time alone with the Father a priority, then we could benefit by doing the same. When I was a teenager, I worked for a man who, from time to time, would call me into his office, pull up a chair right next to me, look straight into my eyes, and say, "Mark, how's your spiritual life?" I was so intimidated that I was afraid not to tell him the truth. How about you? What if I invited you into my office and I sat down next to you, looked straight into your eyes, and asked, "How's your spiritual life?" How would you respond? Are you making any progress, or are you just shuffling along? If it's not what you want it to be, then follow Moses's advice and find satisfaction in the morning in God's unfailing love.

Next, we learn contentment is the secret to putting life into our years. Look at Psalm 90:15: "Make us glad for as many days as you have afflicted us, and for as many years as we have seen evil."

Moses knew all about being afflicted. He didn't ask for the job of leading the children of Israel out of Egypt and toward the Promised Land. He even tried to get out of it at the burning bush, but God would not let him get away. He appointed Moses as the leader, and Moses obeyed the Lord's commands. But this work was not without trouble and difficulty. For example, at one critical moment when things had gotten especially burdensome, Moses cried out to God, asking,

> Why have you dealt ill with your servant? And why have I not found favor in your sight, that you lay the burden of all this people on me? Did I conceive all this people? Did I give them birth, that you should say to me, "Carry them in your bosom, as a nurse carries a nursing child," to the land that you swore to give their fathers? Where am I to get meat to give to all this people? For they weep before me and say, "Give us meat, that we may eat." I am not able to carry all this people alone; the burden is too heavy for me. If you will treat me like this, kill me at once, if I find favor in your sight, that I may not see my wretchedness" (Numbers 11:11–15).

Do you ever feel this way? Have you ever felt the burden was so great you just couldn't carry on? If you have, then you have a friend in Moses. He experienced the same emotions, yet he says in this psalm attributed to him, "Make us glad for as many days as you have afflicted us, and for as many years as we have seen evil" (Psalm 90:15).

Moses, through many years of difficulty, learned contentment is the secret to putting life into your years. This doesn't mean things are always going to go great for you. It doesn't mean things will always go your way. It doesn't mean you are always going to get everything you want. It means you have learned to move beyond all of these temporal issues and discovered what Moses discovered—that God is the source of true peace, contentment, and happiness.

I read a story that illustrates this truth. There was a man who lived in a tiny hut with his wife, two small children, and his elderly parents. He tried to be patient and kind, but the noise and crowded conditions wore him down. In desperation, he consulted with the village wise man. "Do you have a rooster?" asked the wise man.

"Yes," he replied.

"Keep the rooster in the hut with your family, and come see me again in a week." The next week, the man returned and told the wise man that living conditions were worse than ever, with the rooster crowing and making a mess of the hut. "Do you have a cow?" asked the wise man. The man nodded reluctantly. "Take the cow into the hut with you, and come and see me in a week." Over the next several weeks, the man, on the advice of the wise man—made room for a goat, two dogs, and his brother's children. Finally, he couldn't take it anymore, and in a fit of anger, he kicked out all of the animals and guests, leaving only his wife, his children, and his parents. The home suddenly became spacious and quiet, and everyone lived happily ever after.

Contentment in life is based more upon attitude than upon our circumstances. Some of the happiest people I've ever met were living in cinder block homes with dirt floors in Indonesia. I couldn't get over how happy and content they seemed to be under these circumstances. The Bible declares, "Godliness with contentment is great gain" (1 Timothy 6:6).

Paul said, "I have learned to be content whatever the circumstances" (Philippians 4:11).

Are you tired of chasing the wind? Are you tired of being tired? Discover the secret Moses discovered many centuries ago, and find your satisfaction in God.

This brings us to the final suggestion I want to make in this chapter on living a full and meaningful life. The third suggestion is to make your life count. In other words, don't waste your life on things that will not last for all eternity. I've worked with lots of senior adults through the years. I can assure you, the happiest ones are the ones who can see the big picture. Look at Psalm 90: 16–17. Moses writes,

> Let your work be shown to your servants, and your
> glorious power to their children. Let the favor of the
> Lord our God be upon us, and establish the work
> of our hands upon us; yes, establish the work of our
> hands!(Psalm 90:16–17).

Do you want to establish the work of your hands? Do you want to leave a lasting legacy others can follow? If you do, then get involved in activities that will last for all eternity. Spend time investing in your children and grandchildren. Find significant volunteer work to do in your community. Help your church to be the best it can be for God's glory. Pray for your pastor and staff. Find ways to lend a helping hand. Be supportive and cooperative. Understand it is not all about you. Ask God to show you the work He wants you to be involved in, and then get busy doing the work.

Carefully read the next two chapters. In the "Challenges" chapter, the individuals are focused upon themselves and their personal likes and dislikes. As a result, they were very difficult to be around, and often were a hindrance to the ministry. In contrast, chapter 6, "The Reward" is filled with people who are focused on others. They use their talents, gifts, and abilities to bless others. They put life into their years by being instruments God could use to further His kingdom work. The favor of the Lord was upon the work of their hands. I think you know which group I hope you will join. We put life into our years by giving ourselves away in service to others.

CHAPTER FIVE

🔲🔲🔲🔲🔲🔲🔲🔲🔲🔲🔲🔲🔲🔲🔲🔲🔲🔲🔲🔲🔲🔲🔲🔲🔲🔲🔲🔲🔲🔲

Challenges

I'll never forget the experience I'm about to relate as long as I live. I was settling into my office after only a few months of work in my first pastorate. There was a knock at the door, and I welcomed one of our older ladies into my office. We spoke for just a moment, and then she asked for a sheet of paper. I opened a drawer and handed her the paper. She took the piece of paper, violently crumpled it up in front of me, and then with all her might hurled it against the wall. She then turned to me and said, "That's how you make me feel!"

I was taken aback by this dramatic demonstration, and I asked her to explain what I had done to produce such a passionate reaction. She said, "Last night in the meeting, when you said the nursery looks horrible, and we need to clean it up and completely redo it if we ever expect to reach any young families, you hurt my feelings. You have no idea how hard we have already worked on the nursery. You'd think we've never done anything, until you showed up!" I apologized and asked for her forgiveness, but the truth was the nursery did look horrible. It desperately needed to be remodeled

I learned a valuable lesson through this experience. You have to use tact and good judgment when you're working with people.

As the saying goes, "You catch more bees with honey than you do with vinegar." You never want people to think you are discounting everything they have done before you came along. The extra effort of working behind the scenes, building relationships, and bringing people along with you will pay rich dividends over time.

Working with senior adults can be challenging. It requires patience and understanding. Most of the seniors I've worked with through the years grew up during the Great Depression. Also, many of them lived through World War II. They have experienced more significant changes during their lifetimes than most people have for centuries. Many have handled these changes very well, while others struggle to get along in the modern world. It is helpful to take all of this into consideration when you meet with resistance and even outright conflict.

Considering my love for senior adults, you might mistakenly assume I have never had to deal with any conflict or difficulty in working with people in this age group, but you would be greatly mistaken. I've had more than my share of challenges working with these individuals, but I never once thought about asking them to leave the church. This is a rookie mistake some pastors make, and then they have to suffer the consequences of this unfortunate decision.

For example, I once followed in the footsteps of a pastor who was relieved of his duties because he attempted to make significant changes too rapidly. I heard the story numerous times of how the people showed up for church one particular Sunday, and the choir loft had been cleared of chairs and all of the pulpit furniture was missing, and in their place were a drum set, amps, guitars, and a music stand. The pastor boldly announced, "This is how it's going to be from now on, and if you don't like it, then don't let the door hit you on the way out!" Guess who was out the door within less than a month? It wasn't the seniors who had been there for years. It was the young pastor, who had moved too quickly and had tried to brazenly force his agenda upon the congregation.

We eventually had drums and guitars as part of the worship service, but these things were gradually added over time. However, this change wasn't achieved without difficulty, especially in light of these previous events. It seems that the patriarch of the church had lived a wild and uproarious life when he was younger, and unfortunately, upbeat and lively music reminded him of the juke joints and nightclubs he had frequented during those days.

This all came to a head one Sunday evening when people started clapping along as we were singing, "Victory in Jesus." He suddenly stood up, threw his arms up in the air, and with disgust on his face, stormed out of the sanctuary. I've never considered "Victory in Jesus" to be an offensive song. Therefore, I was very surprised by his actions. Apparently, he wasn't offended by the song, but by the clapping. His wife later sent me a note listing all the verses in the Bible that mention clapping in a derogatory manner. He eventually came back. We continued to clap, but he was not happy about it. He repeatedly told me, "I don't want any of that honky-tonk music in this church!" I don't think they are singing "Victory in Jesus" down at the local tavern, but I might be mistaken. I haven't been to one lately.

Seniors can be peculiar, set in their ways, and resistant to change, but I have to remind myself that I can also be the same way. Having good people skills is an essential character trait every leader must develop. I've developed mine through the school of hard knocks, and I'm sure you have too. For instance, in one of my first business meetings, I made a motion, and nobody seconded it! Can you imagine? I can't even remember what it was I thought we ought to do, but I made the motion and silence followed. Everyone was nervously looking around at each other, but no one spoke up. Finally, I said, "Well, I guess this is something we don't want to do. Let's move on …" It was embarrassing, but I learned to never go into a business meeting without talking to key leaders and letting them make the motions.

The first major conflict I ever dealt with directly with a senior adult was over money. Admittedly, the church was small, but I felt we needed to follow a budget. Up until my arrival, standard operating procedure at the church had been for the treasurer to control the money. He was an elderly Irishman, and he was accustomed to getting the final say on how the money was spent.

For instance, I quickly discerned that if the expense was something he approved of, then there was always money to do the work. However, if the idea was not to his liking, then we didn't have money to do it. I was not happy with this arrangement. Therefore, I invited him to my office to discuss the finances, and things quickly escalated. I proposed adopting a church budget and then spending the funds however the church decided. His face began to get redder and redder. He was highly insulted I would suggest another way of doing things. He snarled, "We've done it this way long before you got here, and we will be doing it this way long after you are gone!" He really let his Irish temper get the best of him. I even noticed he was balling up his fist. I actually thought he was going to hit me.

I didn't argue with him, and I didn't mention this encounter to anyone else until the next meeting of our church council, of which he was a member. I began my portion of the meeting by stating, "I would like to propose we adopt a church budget, but I've been told this is not the way you do things. In fact, I've been told this is how you've done things, and this is how you will be doing them long after I'm gone. But I can't operate this way. We need to spend money on the things we approve of as a church and not leave it up to one individual to decide. So I'm going to step outside and let you folks discuss how you want to operate." As I said this, all eyes in the room turned toward the fiery Irishman. Apparently, he had used these same tactics in the past.

Later that evening, I was approached by our huge African American deacon, who was the assistant principal at a local high school in charge of discipline. He said in his deep baritone voice, "He won't be messing with you anymore!" I will also say, to his credit, the Irishman came to me and apologized for his behavior. He even asked me if I wanted him and his wife to leave the church.

I told him, "No, I don't want you to leave, but I do want you to work with me."

We never had any more problems during my tenure at the church. In fact, his wife was very upset with me when I left the church. She exclaimed, "You were supposed to be the one to do my funeral!"

Money can bring out the best and the worst in people, especially among folks who had to live through the Great Depression. They want to save everything, and they don't want to spend money on anything. Unfortunately, this attitude can sometimes have tragic consequences. Many years ago, before the advent of iPads, iPhones, and digital everything, people used this thing called a "camera." There was even a neat device called a Polaroid camera, which would actually shoot the photo out the bottom of the device when you took a photograph.

It was time for vacation Bible school, and one church member, an extremely excited young mother who just happened to be a new Christian, wanted to help. So we gave her the Polaroid camera and asked her to take photographs of the kids. She was young. She was new. She was excited. She was so happy to be able to help that she took lots of photographs. She took so many photographs that one of the older women severely chastised her for wasting all of the expensive film. She was so hurt by this experience that she left the church and never came back. The price of a roll of film is not worth being a stumbling block to a new Christian. Jesus once said, "Whoever causes one of these little ones who believe in me to sin, it would be better for him if a great millstone were hung around his neck and he were thrown into the sea" (Mark 9:42).

Along these same lines, we had a workday at the large church where I served as a youth pastor. I was tasked with cleaning out a closet in one of the adult Sunday school classrooms. I went through the closet, and I threw away everything that I deemed to be useless. Later that afternoon, I was walking by the dumpster, and I was surprised to see one of the senior adult ladies actually in the dumpster. She had somehow climbed into the dumpster, and she was holding up a Styrofoam head, one of those you might sometimes see a wig sitting on in a thrift store. She held it over her head and angrily shouted, "Who threw this away?"

I timidly answered, "I did."

She then castigated me for throwing away a perfectly good Styrofoam head, and she said they used it for something—but for the life of me, I can't remember what she said they used it for. I was flabbergasted that she was over in the dumpster going through the items we had thrown away.

Many years later, at another church, we rented a two-ton dumpster so we could go through and clear out a tremendous amount of clutter. Amazingly, this huge dumpster was not large enough to hold everything. So we put caution tape around the huge pile of rubble until we could get another dumpster delivered to haul away the rest of the junk. A long line formed of seniors asking for items in the junk pile that Sunday after church. We might be tempted to laugh in our throwaway society, but folks who lived through the Great Depression can teach us a lot about the value of thrift and needless waste.

However, sometimes things can get downright ridiculous. Some seniors are very resistant to change, not because there is anything wrong with the proposed change, but because it's very different from what they are used to. My favorite story related to this happened while I was pastoring a church in the San Francisco Bay Area. I enlisted one of our men, a very talented woodworker, to build me a smaller pulpit. The pulpit in this church was so huge we had to lay it on its side whenever we had a baptism, so people could see the baptistery. I always jokingly said I felt like I was standing behind the hood of a big Buick every time I would preach. When we had a children's program, we had to move it out of the auditorium. I was using a music stand while the gentleman was building me a new pulpit. This continued for about three weeks, until one Sunday, an older lady approached me and asked, "When are we going to move the pulpit back into place?" I enthusiastically told her that we were not, because a man was building me a new one.

She said, "Well, pastor, it's just not church without that pulpit."

I replied, "C'mon now, you don't really think Jesus had a pulpit when He gave the Sermon on the Mount, do you?"

She shot back, "I know He did, and I have pictures to prove it!"

I'm usually good at maintaining my composure, but when she said this I couldn't help it—I burst out laughing. I said, "Well, if you have pictures to prove it, I sure would like to see them." She later brought me some Sunday school drawings that they do for children, with Jesus standing in the temple behind some type of lectern someone had drawn. But the damage was done. She never forgave me for laughing at her. She was holding onto tradition for the sake of tradition.

This incident leads me to a much more serious discussion of times when seniors have seriously jeopardized our ability to move forward as a church. Holding onto tradition for the sake of tradition can be detrimental to the Lord's work. Let me give a few examples.

A number of years ago, I was the pastor of a church that was so small we didn't have any children. We didn't have any children, but we had a plan. We remodeled the nursery (crumpled paper story), and we designated a particular Sunday for people to work in it, just in case someone made their way to our church with young children. Not long into this arrangement, a young couple showed up for our Sunday service with two beautiful children. This was the answer to our prayers. We had been praying for God to help us reach out to the many young families living in our community, and this couple came with their two precious little ones.

I greeted them at the door, and at the same time turned to someone and said, "Please run and get Linda Lou." It was her Sunday to be in the nursery per our arrangement. My plan was to keep this family occupied to give Linda Lou time to make her way to the nursery before we arrived with the children. Regrettably, the best laid plans of mice and men often go awry. Just a moment later, the front double doors of the sanctuary violently swung open, and Linda Lou stomped past us. As she passed, she said, with clear agitation in her voice, "I'll do it this time, pastor, but don't ever ask me again!" Please understand she had agreed to this in theory, when there were no children to watch, but now that it came time for action, she was clearly unwilling to help. The young mother immediately tensed up and said, "Oh my, is there a problem?"

I replied, "It appears there might be. Why don't you have the kids stay with you during the service? I love children, and I'm sure they will be fine in the service."

Of course, the young couple never came back, but I tracked them down a couple of weeks later and profusely apologized for what had transpired. The young mother compassionately exclaimed, "Oh, pastor, don't worry about it. My father is a pastor, and I felt so sorry for you."

Fortunately, the church was later blessed with an older couple who had a genuine love for children. They volunteered to stay in the nursery almost every Sunday. The church began to grow, and we were blessed with a number of children, even one family with triplets! It all happened because an older couple saw an area of need and decided to meet this need. Unlike Linda Lou, who had helped us lose the first couple God sent our way, this couple blessed our church with willing hearts and generous spirits.

I still remember what this very kind lady said to me one day. She pulled me aside and whispered, "No offense, pastor, but we have heard thousands of sermons. We believe working in the nursery is where the Lord wants to use us at this time." She was absolutely right, and the Lord richly blessed their efforts. Senior adults with their hearts in the right place can be a tremendous blessing to any congregation.

However, if we are not careful, we can develop a sense of ownership and entitlement, which can hurt a church's efforts to reach out. For instance, I had to speak with a sweet older lady at one of the churches I served, because she kept telling our guests they were sitting in her seat. Obviously, it's where she had sat for many years, but the seat did not belong to her. I tried to help her see how off-putting this behavior was to people who were visiting our church.

Similarly, we once planned an Easter egg hunt in a local park to try to attract young families to our church. We intentionally sought out a park instead of doing the event at our church, in an effort to be out in our community. We hoped we would reach some new families or at least make contact with families who might start coming to our church. I thought we had clearly communicated these motives to everyone, but apparently we hadn't, because just as we were about to begin the hunt, something happened that threw a damper upon the entire experience.

A number of us arrived early and got everything set up. We prepared the refreshments. We set up for the games. We scattered the eggs. We were ready. The kids were all lined up. I was about to give the signal to start when a beautiful young couple walked by, just the type of couple we were trying to reach. One of their children saw the brightly colored eggs and reached down to pick one up. To my horror, one of our older ladies screamed, "Don't touch that! It's for our Sunday school kids!" I wanted to die. She had completely missed the point. This was the reason we were out in the park in the first place. The eggs were not just for our Sunday school kids; they were for any child who might like to have one. Needless to say, we didn't pick up any new contacts through this event.

Ironically, I experienced something very similar once on a Saturday morning. I decided to ride my bicycle to the church to spend some time in prayer and look over my sermon notes for Sunday. Obviously, I didn't have on my usual Sunday morning attire. I was wearing shorts and a T-shirt. I also was wearing my bicycle helmet and sunglasses. At the precise moment I was dismounting from my bicycle and walking toward the front of the church, an older ladies' prayer group was exiting the fellowship hall. I'm sure they had been praying for our efforts to reach our community for Christ, but this didn't prevent one of the women from screaming at me, "Hey, get away from here! What are you doing?"

I calmly took off my helmet and sunglasses, and I said to her in front of all the others, "Is that any way to talk to your pastor?" They all laughed; but then I said, "What if I had been someone from the community walking up to see what time the service started?" Unfortunately, we sometimes get so overprotective of the building, we forget about the souls we are trying to reach.

This story brings me back to a difficult patriarch in one of my first churches. When I first went to the church, the church was renting space to a Chinese congregation. They met in the fellowship hall on Sunday afternoons for worship. The good news is that this church grew large enough to buy their own facility, and we were making plans for their departure.

At the same time, we were approached by a Korean congregation who wanted to rent some space. However, instead of worshipping in the fellowship hall, they asked to rent the sanctuary. It was very important to them to worship in the sanctuary. I was presenting this request to the deacons. Yes, regrettably, the difficult patriarch was a deacon. I began to explain the request to the men, and Mr. Difficult spoke up. He said, "I didn't mind having those people in the fellowship hall, but I do not want to have them in the sanctuary."

This blatantly racist comment infuriated me, and so I replied, "Well, Mr. Smith (name changed to protect the guilty), what do you think heaven is going to be like?"

He slammed both fists down on the table and shouted, "This ain't heaven!" He stormed out, and this time he didn't come back for a long, long time. It's sad when we let our prejudices and pride of ownership get in the way of the Lord's work. The Korean church came and stayed for a while. Today, they are one of the largest Korean congregations in that particular city.

As you can see, I've had more than my share of conflicts, confrontations, and misunderstandings with senior adults, but I love them anyway. I love them anyway because they are part of the flock entrusted to my care. I love them for their wisdom and insight. I love them for their stories. I love them for their long years of dedication and service. It seems to me there are two types of old people—those who grow bitter and those who get better. Some people age gracefully, while others enter the later stages of life kicking and screaming. Some are a tremendous blessing, while others are tremendously draining and burdensome. The apostle Paul said near the end of his life,

> For I am already being poured out as a drink offering, and the time of my departure has come. I have fought the good fight, I have finished the race, I have kept the faith. Henceforth there is laid up for me the crown of righteousness, which the Lord, the righteous judge, will award to me on that day, and not only to me but also to all who have loved his appearing (2 Timothy 4:6–8).

We all want to someday hear the Lord declare, "Well done, good and faithful servant."

I hope we all will be able to say with Paul, "I have fought the good fight, I have finished the race, I have kept the faith." Please do whatever you have to do to be a blessing instead of a burden to those around you. The next chapter might give you a few ideas of how to make this happen in your life.

CHAPTER SIX

5555555555555555555555555555555555555555555

The Reward

I love the way Max Lucado concludes his book *The Applause of Heaven*. He describes this beautiful heavenly scene as only he can:

> You may not have noticed it, but you are closer to home than ever before. Each moment is a step taken. Each breath is a page turned. Each day is a mile marked, a mountain climbed. You are closer to home than you've ever been. Before you know it, your appointed arrival time will come; you'll descend the ramp and enter the City. You'll see faces waiting for you. You'll hear your name spoken by those who love you. And, maybe, just maybe— in the back, behind the crowds—the One who would rather die than live without you will remove his pierced hands from his heavenly robe and … applaud.[16]

---

[16] Max Lucado, *The Applause of Heaven* (Nashville: Thomas Nelson Publishing, 1990), p. 190.

If we want to hear the applause of heaven someday, then it matters how we live today. I shared some of the challenges I've had while working with senior adults in the previous chapter. In this chapter, I want to look at the rewards of working with and encouraging people in this age group.

I still remember the very first Bible study I ever taught with a group of senior adults. I was serving on the staff at Woodmont Baptist Church in Florence, Alabama, as the youth pastor. However, when I graduated from college, the church expanded my role. I became the minister of youth and senior adults. How often have you seen this title? I thoroughly enjoyed this experience. I eventually came to view it as having two youth groups; one was just a lot older than the other.

However, when I first started working with the seniors, I was very nervous about leading my first Bible study. I couldn't imagine having anything to say that they hadn't already heard many times before. Therefore, I truthfully shared with the group my apprehensions about trying to teach them anything. One of the sweet older ladies spoke up and said, "Honey, don't be nervous; we are all still learning just like you." At some point in life, we all make a transition and most of the people we are listening to are younger. I pray that God will give us the attitude expressed by this gracious lady and have the grace to learn from those coming along behind us. I've had the good fortune to rub shoulders with numerous kind and gracious senior citizens over the course of my life, and I'm grateful for their influence.

My earliest experience with seniors was with my grandparents, and even great-grandparents. I had the good fortune of having three of my great-grandparents live until I was in high school. I even remember and was present for the fiftieth wedding anniversaries of my great-grandparents, my grandparents, and my parents. So I have been blessed in tremendous ways through my immediate family. I readily acknowledge this, but my experiences go far beyond those of my godly upbringing.

For instance, Martha Willis had a tremendous impact upon my life. She has climbed the Great Wall of China, traveled the Amazon River, and battled mosquitoes in Alaska. And she has done it all in the name of Jesus. Following her retirement in 1982, she went on nineteen home mission projects and seventeen foreign ones. In 1995, she earned the Volunteer of the Year Award, given by the Alabama Baptist State Convention. She traveled to Korea, South America, Africa, Australia, England, Mexico, Spain, Russia, and China to tell people about Christ.

I share all of this with you because before she became a world-traveling missionary, Mrs. Willis was the vacation Bible school director at Kilpatrick Baptist Church, where my father was the pastor. In this role, she made a big impression on my life. I still remember her leading us through the opening ceremony, helping us recite the pledges, teaching us our memory verses, and telling us about our missionaries around the world. I will always be indebted to Mrs. Willis for helping to mold and shape my life for Christ. She went home to her reward a few years ago, but her life reminds us that we never know what God will do with the seeds we plant today.

Donald Drain was not very well known outside of the small farming community where he lived all of his life, but he left his mark on my life. I remember many Sunday evenings spent under a tree at Mt. Flat Baptist Church with Mr. Drain. He would say to the group of boys gathered around him that he didn't know much, but then he would read to us from the Bible and talk to us about it. I don't think he ever thought he was accomplishing very much out under that old oak tree, but several of the young pupils from his class ended up being pastors! The lesson from his life is that we should never underestimate the power of God in our lives. We might not think we are having much impact, but only time will tell how God might use us and bless our efforts. So be encouraged! I'm sure you are having a greater impact than you can ever imagine.

I can still vividly remember Dr. George Ricker, the director of Shocco Springs Baptist Assembly in Talladega, Alabama, the camp where I worked as a teenager. One day he called me into his office, pulled up a chair very close to mine, and looked directly into my eyes. He began, "So, Mark, how's it going in your walk with the Lord?" He challenged me over and over that summer to live my life for Christ and to make a difference for Him. It was four years later, while working at the same camp, that I made my commitment to go into the ministry. Dr. Ricker has faithfully checked in on me through the years. I don't believe a year has transpired since I made my commitment to the ministry that Dr. Ricker hasn't called at least once to see how it's going in my walk with the Lord. His faithful consistency in my life has inspired me to keep reaching higher in my Christian endeavors. Whom are you encouraging to press on in their Christian life?

I also vividly remember an experience I had several years later while I was serving on the staff of Boyd Avenue Baptist Church in Casper, Wyoming. I was taking a group of kids to summer camp on Casper Mountain. It was a very tough week. The camp conditions were very rugged, to say the least. The boys and I slept under a circus tent in our sleeping bags on wooden pallets. It was freezing cold at night; we sometimes woke up to the sound of water flowing under the pallets. We didn't get much rest. I remember being very tired in the chapel one afternoon when an elderly lady pulled me aside and read a passage of scripture to me. She read Jeremiah 1:5–8:

> "Before I formed you in the womb I knew you, and before you were born I consecrated you; I appointed you a prophet to the nations." Then I said, "Ah, Lord God! Behold, I do not know how to speak, for I am only a youth." But the Lord said to me, "Do not say, 'I am only a youth'; for to all to whom I send you, you shall go, and whatever I command you, you shall speak. Do not be afraid of them, for I am with you to deliver you, declares the Lord."

She described how the Lord had impressed this passage upon her heart for me. I don't even know her name, but God used this godly older lady to confirm His calling upon my life. I went away strengthened and encouraged by her kind words. Whom can you build up today by speaking an encouraging word into their life?

Mr. Carlton Davis impressed me with his servant's heart while I was serving on the staff of a large church in Florence, Alabama. I remember even being told in a staff meeting once, "Mr. Davis doesn't want any public recognition for the things he does." It was easy to see why, because he did so many things. However, the thing about him I remember most was his willingness to lock up after services. The church had a very large facility, and this was a time-consuming task, going around to all of the buildings and making sure everything was secure.

Mr. Davis was a widower, and I once heard him say, "I have no reason to rush home. I'm happy to go around and check all of the doors. It's an easy ministry for me." Obviously, it wasn't easy. It's a thankless job for which many churches struggle to find someone willing to take on the responsibility, but this kindhearted senior stepped forward to do this job. His willingness to serve in this capacity freed up the staff to be involved in other activities. I've always fondly remembered his faithfulness and been challenged by his example. I'm also, in my small way, giving him the public recognition he did not want but so richly deserved.

"No, pastor, please let me make the motion." These words were sweet music to my ears. The first church I served as pastor was so small we didn't even have a pianist. This is where Era stepped in and made a significant commitment. Era was a dedicated senior adult with a heart of gold. She had limited experience playing the piano when she was younger, but it had been many, many years since she had touched a keyboard. She signed up and started taking piano lessons at her advanced age just so we could have someone to play during the music portions of our services. She would sometimes struggle, but we all admired her grit and determination.

This went on for a number of months, until a young college student began attending our services. It was brought to my attention that this young lady was an excellent pianist, but I was worried about Era. How would she respond to being replaced, after she had gone to so much trouble to help us out during a difficult time? I was concerned about hurting her feelings and how she would react, but I had forgotten about her heart of gold. I approached her with fear and trepidation. I told her about the young lady, and I gingerly asked her what she thought about allowing her to play during the services. She smiled and gushed, "Pastor, please don't worry about it. I'm happy God has answered my prayers. Let me make the motion in the business meeting." I will never forget her courage in stepping up when we needed her, and her gracious willingness to step aside when God provided another solution. I learned valuable lessons from her about the willingness to do what it takes, and the humility to step aside when a job is done.

Leona Davidson will always be remembered for her sacrificial willingness to help others. She contracted a rare form of cancer and volunteered for a series of experimental treatments at Stanford University Medical Center. I was visiting with her once during one of her numerous hospital stays. I asked her how she was doing, and she replied, "Pastor, if going through all of this will help one other person, then it will all be worth it." I will always remember this selfless act of charity and goodwill.

This also reminds me of the cheerful greeting I received from my friend Juanita one day in the ICU. She was having complications from a recent surgery. She had already been told she didn't have long to live. She was hooked up to all kinds of machines, and it seemed like she was covered in IVs. But I'll never forget her reply when I walked into the room and asked how she was doing. Her face brightened, and she exclaimed, "Well, pastor, it's just another day to praise the Lord!" She was always one of my favorites, because of her big, kind heart.

A few years earlier, Donnie began attending our church and

was very eager to get involved. There was only one problem. Donnie did not have a car, and the bus service was highly unreliable. But upon further examination, I discovered that Donnie lived in the same apartment complex as the aforementioned Juanita, one of our faithful senior adults. I called Juanita and explained the situation. I asked her if she would mind if Donnie rode to church with her each week. Juanita was a very gracious "Okie" with a gift for hospitality. She replied that she would love to give Donnie a ride. I was very proud of myself for solving this transportation problem, but about a month later Donnie approached me after church one Sunday and announced, "I can't ride with that woman anymore!"

Naturally, I asked, "Why not?"

She replied, "She ran every red light on the way to church this morning!"

I made other arrangements for Donnie to get home from church. A few days later, I asked Juanita if I could ride with her to a restaurant following our senior adult Bible study. I wanted to see for myself if Donnie's concerns were valid. Juanita ran every light on the way to the restaurant! Understandably, this was the beginning of the end for her driver's license. Her spirit was willing, but her eyes were weak!

"This is my adopted grandson" was the way Hazel Philips would always introduce me to the staff, attendants, and anyone else who would listen to her, when I would stop by for a visit at the beautiful Masonic Home in Union City, California. Of course, this was not true, but I was glad to be considered a member of the family. Hazel and her husband, Guy, raised several boys, and a number of them grew up to be pastors. She also had a grandson who was a missionary. Therefore, I was honored to be included in such a godly clan.

Hazel was one of the most dedicated and committed Christians I've ever had the pleasure of being around. She told me, on numerous occasions, how she started teaching Sunday school when she was seventeen years old. Her pastor approached her about teaching a class of young girls. She replied, "Pastor, I can't teach. I don't have any education."

He said, "It doesn't take education. It takes dedication."

She took him at his word and began to teach. She was still teaching while I served as her pastor, when she was well into her nineties. She was the epitome of dedication. In fact, when her mind started slipping near the end of her life, no one, including myself, had the heart to tell her she couldn't teach anymore. So the ladies in her class all made sure they had studied their lesson, and if she got off track one of them would jump in and help her to get back on course. So, thank you, Hazel. You were an inspiration to everyone, including your adopted grandson.

Mr. Eugene Greenfield moved to California from Table Rock Mountain in Arkansas many years ago. He would often talk with me about his childhood memories of growing up on the mountain, but what will forever be etched in my mind about Mr. Greenfield was his love and devotion to his wife, Thelma. Thelma suffered from many physical ailments in the latter part of her life. She even lost the ability to walk the last couple years of her life and had to be placed in a nursing home. Mr. Greenfield would get up early every morning to go to the nursing home, and he would stay with his wife all day. He would stay until after she had her dinner and got ready for bed; then he would collect his things and go home. He did this every day until the day she died. I've never known a man who exhibited more love and devotion to his wife than Mr. Greenfield did. I praise God for his example of unconditional love and commitment. We need more men like him today.

Ralph Harvey was cut from the same cloth. I met Ralph when I accepted the call to become the pastor of Sherwood Baptist Church in Huntsville, Alabama. Mr. Harvey was a mild-mannered, unassuming man. He was a widower and primarily kept to himself. I didn't really know much about him, but I heard from others that he had a ministry over at one of the local nursing homes. One day, he called and invited me to go with him to the nursing home, and my eyes were opened to the love and dedication of this godly man.

About twenty years earlier, his wife had been sent to this nursing home to recover from some sort of surgery. It developed into an extended stay. So Ralph had an opportunity to meet many of the residents. He was alarmed to discover that many of the folks had no one to visit with them, and this touched Ralph's heart. He began making rounds in the nursing home, and he became sort of a self-appointed chaplain.

He continued this ministry even after the death of his wife. This included leading a small worship service at the home each Sunday morning. As I walked down the hallway of the nursing home with Mr. Harvey, I felt like I was walking alongside a celebrity. Many of the patients would call out his name. Others would step forward to give him a hug. You could see the genuine love and affection in their eyes for this godly man who cared enough to come and spend time with them. I stand in awe of Mr. Harvey and his faithful consistency in serving the people at this nursing home. He has spent his life in service to others.

Dee Good, a lovely lady from Del Cerro Baptist Church in San Diego, California, overcame her aversion to nursing homes by beginning to carry her Pomeranian dogs to cheer up the patients. Her story is told in an article titled, "Pom Tuesdays," in *Guideposts Magazine* dated September 2014. In the article, Dee is quoted as saying,

> I was reading the newspaper at the kitchen table when a photo caught my eye—adorable dogs being petted by senior citizens.
>
> "Visit from Locals and Their Dogs Brings Joy to Nursing Home Residents," the headline read.
>
> *Good for them,* I thought, shuddering. Quickly, I turned the page.

That's when I heard it. A voice. Male. Not Danny [her husband], who was still down in the basement. Not anyone I recognized.

You have cute little dogs, the voice said. You can do that too.

Wow, I'm hearing things, I thought. *I must be really tired ...*

Dee, you can do that. There it was again, more emphatic.

"God, if that's you, you're going to have to give me something else to do," I said. "I can't do nursing homes, remember?" Not only was I hearing voices, I was talking back!

Yes, you can. This time it was more than a statement. It was a command.

"Fine, I'll do it!" I blurted.

Silence. The voice was gone.[17]

The rest of the article describes how Dee overcame her distaste for nursing homes, genuinely loved the residents, and became a consistent blessing to others. I was so proud to be her pastor.

I've missed Bob Miller practically every day since he and his wife packed up and moved away, from Gilroy to Pismo Beach, a number of years ago. Bob's positive attitude and willingness to serve were contagious. He volunteered countless hours at the church, where I was the pastor, and his response to the question, "How are

---

[17] Dee Good, "Pom Tuesdays," *Guideposts Magazine*, September 2014.

you doing?" was always the same: "Outstanding!" However, what I've missed the most about Bob Miller through the years is his wise counsel. Bob had a knack for looking at all sides of an issue and clearly seeing the potential outcomes of every decision. I can't even count the number of times I sat down with Bob and he helped me work through the ramifications of a decision.

I wish all pastors could have men like Bob Miller in their lives, people who give wise godly counsel, without criticism and without judgment. Bob was more than a thinker. He was a peacemaker who always kept the big picture in mind. He embodied the words of Paul to the Philippians:

> Finally, brothers, whatever is true, whatever is honorable, whatever is just, whatever is pure, whatever is lovely, whatever is commendable, if there is any excellence, if there is anything worthy of praise, think about these things. What you have learned and received and heard and seen in me—practice these things, and the God of peace will be with you (Philippians 4:8–9).

Churches are sometimes filled with too many people who want to argue and criticize. We need more men like Bob Miller who help us work toward thoughtful and peaceful solutions. Here is a great question to ponder: Are you a troublemaker or a peacemaker? Bob was a peacemaker, and I miss him.

In the same way, Ken Lowe was a tremendous gift God sent my way at the church I served in San Diego. Ken has an MBA from Stanford University. He spent the early part of his career working for the prestigious McKinsey & Company, the premier management consulting firm in the world. Then he lead his own management consulting firm, exclusively for lawyers, from 1984 until he retired in 2002.

His IQ is off the charts. He once told me he and his sister read every book in his hometown library during his younger years. He also spent time as a child trying to memorize every word in the dictionary. He is brilliant and served as a tremendous asset whenever I needed someone to talk with about an issue. Sure, he was analytical and thorough, but he had a tremendous heart for God. He was and continues to be an incredible blessing to me. I'm so grateful for men like Bob and Ken, who use their wisdom to further God's kingdom.

Anna Dewey was a quiet, unassuming individual who could always make you feel special. She was also a deeply principled woman; she loved her country and worked hard to protect the freedoms and promote the virtues that have made this country great. I came across a quote I wish I could have shared at her memorial service. It is from the American political leader Adlai Stevenson. Hopefully, she will forgive me for quoting a Democrat, since she was such a staunch conservative, but his quote reaches beyond party lines: "Patriotism is not a short and frenzied burst of emotion, but the tranquil and steady dedication of a life."[18]

I believe this quote is a fitting description of Anna's life. She formed the ladies' VIPs (Volunteers in Politics) organization and made a significant difference in the political landscape of the San Diego region, as was evidenced by the number of dignitaries present at her memorial service. We heard from a sitting congressman, a former congressman who once ran for president, a former state legislator, and a current assemblyman. It was an impressive display of the difference one life can make. I'm inspired by her courage, and challenged by her life, to remember that patriotism is not a short burst of emotion, but the steady dedication of a life.

I'll never forget the first time I met Jim Nugent. His wife, Loura, served on the pastor search committee, so I had already met her. I first met Jim when they picked us up at the airport in San Diego,

---

[18] Adlai Stevenson, Speech to the American Legion convention, New York City (27 August 1952); as quoted in "Democratic Candidate Adlai Stevenson Defines the Nature of Patriotism" in *Lend Me Your Ears: Great Speeches in History* (2004) by William Safire, pp. 79–80.

when we flew in for the interview weekend at Del Cerro Baptist Church. They were driving Jim's European touring car, and once we all got buckled in, Jim hit the accelerator. The engine revved so that it sounded like a rocket about to blast off. Loura leaned over and said, "Honey, I don't think you have it in gear." Luckily for us this was the case; otherwise, we might have blasted off for the moon!

This was a rather inauspicious beginning for what developed into a wonderful friendship. We shared a common heartbeat for missions. Jim and Loura have spent their lives in service to others. Two of their four children, along with their spouses and children, are on the mission field serving in East Asia. So, they have obviously lived and breathed missions throughout their lifetimes. I understand that while Loura was still working full time, she helped Vietnamese and Cambodian refugees when they first came to this country, but they have especially used their retirement to spread the love of Christ.

After Loura retired in 1993, she began helping the Somali people with their settlement in San Diego. She did this because God moved her heart to show His love and compassion to this displaced group of people. They did this for many years, often asking church members for donations of old furniture. They used their old van to pick these items up and deliver them to families in need.

Just before my arrival at the church in 2009, the church became the primary sponsor for a new work with the Karen people from Myanmar (formerly Burma). The Karen refugees came to call Loura "Pi-Lu," which in their language means, "Grandma." I was amazed by "Pi-Lu" and Jim and their tireless efforts to help these people get settled in their new lives. Many people who now call this country home will always remember them for their love and devotion to the Lord.

I know pastors are not supposed to have favorites, but Millie Shriver will always be one of my favorites for a number of reasons. First, she was just a fun person to be around. She enjoyed humor and seeing the lighter side of life. We hit it off right away once she discovered I also have a good sense of humor. I also enjoyed Millie because she was genuine and real. She had had some struggles in life, and she did not try to hide them. She told me about them right up front when I first met her. I always appreciated this about her. So many people try to hide things from others, especially the pastor, so it's refreshing to meet someone who is so genuine and real.

I also enjoyed Millie because we shared a couple of funny experiences. The first was when I told a story in church one night about visiting one of our elderly ladies in a nursing home. When I started to leave, the flirtatious widow said, "How about a kiss?" So I kissed her on the cheek. I told this story in church, and then the next time I went to see Millie at the senior living facility where she resided, when I started to leave, she lightheartedly pointed to her cheek and said, "How about a kiss?" We would often laugh about this lighthearted moment.

Additionally, I went to see her in the hospital once after she had surgery, and she was hallucinating, seeing big bugs up on the wall and that sort of thing. I played along with it at the time, but we also got a good laugh about this afterward.

The final reason I enjoyed Millie so much was because of the way she was always so encouraging to me. I send out a note to our congregation each Friday that I call, "The Encouraging Word." I would often hear back from Millie thanking me for the encouragement. She would then often provide some encouragement of her own. I want to share some of our correspondence, because it will give you insight into her gift of encouragement. For instance, one Friday I quoted from Laurie Beth Jones' book *Jesus CEO*. She writes, "To shepherd a flock of butterflies, one must stand there in delight."[19]

I wrote, "I've heard church leadership compared to 'Herding cats,' but I like the idea of 'Shepherding butterflies' better. You are God's special creation and it's a joy to walk this road alongside you."

Here is Millie's response to me:

---

[19] Laurie Beth Jones, *Jesus CEO* (New York: Hyperion, 1995), p. 279.

I so appreciated your Encouraging Word on my birthday last Friday—IT WAS REALLY ENCOURAGING!!! Like you, I especially love the phrase ... "To shepherd a flock of butterflies, one must stand there in delight." Leaves a lovely picture imprinted in my mind—one that I can call up and enjoy many times!!!

Love, Millie

I once shared a poem about death entitled, "Shed a Tear for Me." This is what I got back from Millie after that note. She said,

Pastor Mark ... WELL ... You just added one more LOVELY thing in my In-Bin to make me CRY!! Tears, of course, of JOY. Thanks for this lovely poem ... You are such a blessing.

Love, Millie

Here is the poem that made her cry. I share the poem with you not because I wrote it, but because she liked it so much.

Shed a Tear for Me ...

Shed a tear for me when I am gone,
But not for me I'll be home.
Cry for the times when we had fun
And for all the projects left undone.

Shed a tear for me when I am gone,
But not for me I'll be home.
Cry for the times when I made you laugh
And cry for the sake of my better half.

Shed a tear for me when I am gone,
But not for me I'll be home.
Cry for the times when we worked together
And tried to make the world a little better.

Shed a tear for me when I am gone,
But not for me I'll be home.
Cry for my loved ones left behind
And for our efforts to be kind.

Shed a tear for me when I am gone,
But not for me I'll be home.
Cry for the victory that is now mine
I'm with my Savior and I'll be fine.

This is the type of person Millie was deep down inside. She tried to make the most of each day and do whatever she could to brighten someone else's day. This is what I loved about her. Finally, the summer before her death, I wrote a note about securing my burial plots for when my time comes. Millie wrote me a long note back. This is actually the last note I ever received from her:

Pastor Mark,

Thank you so much for sharing these lovely very encouraging words … It reminded me that my parents are buried at Greenwood. Later, but some 15 –20 years ago, "out of the clear blue" I received a solicitation call from Greenwood … and would I like to be buried there as well and could he come out and share info on the final arrangements. I finally made an appointment with the gentleman … I had already pretty much made up my mind to choose cremation … and that was what was arranged (at very modest monthly payments). I didn't go out to see the plot and location for quite some time later. I had a rather rude awakening while looking down at it, "Well, well, well, this is it"—the commemoration of my entire life in this one tiny plot!! I walked over and told my parents "where I was going to be"—I suppose I thought that would comfort them that I chose to be nearby!!

Much, much, later, but while she was still quite young, my daughter, Stephanie, confided, "You know what mom … I'm going to keep your ashes, put them in a brown paper bag, cut out a corner of it and slowly walk on the shoreline where the ashes can trickle out and into the water. That way, you will be in a place you dearly loved, as well as Heaven which you also dearly love." Isn't that a wonderful thought from her—I will treasure it forever. Pastor Mark … thank you for letting me share all of this with you.

Love,

Millie Shriver

P.S. Please continue to pray that my back will soon be healed and I can go out and run thru my favorite field of daisies!!

Are you beginning to see why I love senior adults? Are you beginning to understand why I believe a church is less than it could be without their presence? They have brought so much joy and encouragement into my life. I can't imagine pastoring a church without them. They have been some of my most dependable helpers, thoughtful mentors, enthusiastic encouragers, and faithful friends. I've tried to give you just a snapshot. In reality, this chapter could have gone on for much, much longer. Most of these saints have already gone on to receive their eternal reward. I can only imagine what they are currently experiencing, but I'm quite sure they all heard the applause of heaven when they stepped upon that golden shore for a life well lived. My life is richer, fuller, and happier for having known them.

CHAPTER SEVEN

{decorative border}

Find Us Faithful

A pastor was preaching on going to heaven. He said, "How many of you would like to go to heaven tonight?" And everybody raised their hands, but one little boy in the balcony. He tried again, "How many of you would like to go to heaven?" Everybody did but that one little boy in the balcony, so the pastor said to him, "Son, don't you want to go to heaven?"

The little boy said, "Yeah, someday, but I thought you were gettin' up a load right now!"

We all want to go to heaven someday, but what are we to do in the meantime? How are we supposed to live? I'm convinced that in order to get the most out of life, we must develop an eternal perspective. An eternal perspective helps us to prioritize the things in our lives that are really important. I read recently, "Without a regular reminder that we are eternal, we could easily be drawn into the snare of prioritizing 'things' over people."[20]

Let me draw your attention to a passage of scripture that will help us to gain an eternal perspective. It is found in Hebrews 13

---

[20] Tim Kimmel, *Little House on the Freeway: Help for the Hurried Home* (Colorado Springs: Multnomah Books, 1987), p. 85.

beginning with verse 7: "Remember your leaders, who spoke the word of God to you. Consider the outcome of their way of life and imitate their faith. Jesus Christ is the same yesterday and today and forever" (Hebrews 13:7–8).

A few years ago, I was preaching on the final verse of this text: "Jesus Christ is the same yesterday, and today and forever." This message just happened to be in the evening service, and more than one person pointed out the irony that the title of my Sunday morning message listed in the bulletin for the same Sunday had been, "Change Is Coming!" So we had "Change Is Coming" in the morning and "Jesus Is the Same" in the evening. It was perhaps a scheduling error on my part.

The world is rapidly changing, but we serve the One who is the same yesterday, today, and forever. In other words, we serve the never-changing Jesus in an ever-changing world! Think about how the world has changed during the last one hundred years. My grandfather would have been one hundred years old last September if he were still alive. Think about all of the changes he saw during his lifetime. He went from riding around in a horse and buggy to seeing a man land on the moon! I read that a single weekend edition of *The New York Times* includes more information than the average person in seventeenth-century England encountered over the course of an entire lifetime! Our world is rapidly changing. We are living in the twenty-first century, and it's a time of rapid change and transition.

Admittedly, not all change is bad. Change can often initiate progress and lead to success. For instance, Abraham had to leave Ur before he could step into Canaan. All kinds of change were thrust upon Joseph before he ascended to power in Egypt. And the children of Israel had to leave Egypt before they could step into the Promised Land.

I read where someone defined nostalgia as the fear that God's creativity peaked somewhere in the past. I thought this was an interesting definition of nostalgia, considering the fact that nostalgia is usually described as a longing or a desire for things of the past (like the Israelites longing for the food of Egypt while they were out in the wilderness). It is interesting to think of nostalgia as the fear of God's creativity having peaked in the past, because I believe this idea describes many Christians in our world today. I've seen this type of fear surface when we are challenged to do something new or creative.

I've seen this kind of fear show its face when we've been asked to step out in faith. I've heard this type of fear verbalized when people have said things like, "Well, I just don't know; are you sure about this, pastor? Do you really think this is going to work?" When I hear these sorts of comments, I know we are suffering from the fear that God's creativity peaked in the past. What I've come to understand is that we are hesitant to move forward when our eyes are looking back. Regrettably, too many Christians are living with the nostalgic hope that tomorrow will be yesterday. However, I want to remind you that God's word says, "Jesus Christ is the same yesterday and today and forever" (Hebrews 13:8).

Do you really believe this? I hope you do, because the same Jesus who helped you to succeed in the past is the same Jesus who is ready to help you today, and wants to help you tomorrow. Let me show you why I believe this so strongly. Not all looking back is wrong. In fact, we look to the past for inspiration in the present. In other words, by looking to the past, we find the inspiration we need for present opportunities. Not all nostalgia is bad. In fact, some nostalgia is good. Nostalgia is good if it motivates us to reach higher and strive harder to be what God has called us to be. Look again at Hebrews 13:7. It begins by saying, "Remember your leaders who spoke the word of God to you" (Hebrews 13:7).

We are initially challenged in this passage to remember those who have gone before us and shared the word of God with us. The tense of the word "remember" is such that it means we are not just to remember them, but we are to keep on remembering and never forget those who have gone before us. We remember those who have come before us and worked diligently to provide us with the blessings we enjoy today.

I shared in an earlier chapter how I learned this lesson the hard way at the very first church I pastored, and I've never forgotten it. This was the story of the lady crumpling up the piece of paper and violently flinging it against the wall, if you need a reminder. So I learned very early in my ministry to value and cherish the work of others who have come before us. We are standing on their shoulders and building on the foundation, which has already been laid for us.

So the obvious question is, "Why?" Why is it important to remember those who have gone before? It is important because more often than not, the challenge to remember those who have gone before us is a challenge to get back to the basics. The writer of the book of Hebrews is not challenging the people to remember their leaders because they were extremely eloquent or because they were wonderfully gifted or because they were extraordinarily compassionate. The text says, "Remember your leaders who *spoke the word of God to you*." The writer is challenging us to remember the faithful men and women who have gone before us and have shared the words of life with us.

Where would we be today if someone had not taken the time to share the word of God with us? Think about this for a moment. If I were to ask you, "Who is the one person that has had the greatest impact on your Christian life?" what would you say? How would you answer this question? I'm sure someone immediately comes to mind. Who is it for you? It might be a parent, a grandparent, a Sunday school teacher, a pastor, a youth minister, a friend, a college minister … the list could go on and on, but we are challenged in this passage to remember them.

I want to also challenge you to think of this: our greatest legacy will be those who live eternally because of our efforts. The greatest remembrance we could ever hope for in this life is for someone to look back on our life and say, "He influenced me to follow Christ." "She helped me to find Jesus." "He made a difference in my life by introducing me to Jesus Christ." We look to the past for inspiration in the present.

We might look to the past for inspiration, but we live in the present, in the twenty-first century. This is why our text goes on to declare, "Jesus Christ is the same yesterday, and today." In other words, the same Jesus who healed the sick, opened the eyes of the blind, made the lame to walk, and raised the dead to life … this same Jesus is ready to help us today if we will walk by faith. This passage challenges us to remember and keep on remembering our leaders who spoke the word of God to us, and to consider the outcome of their way of life. "Consider" literally means to "look at again and again."

So, why is it important to consider how people behaved in the past? The answer is because these people not only had good things to say, but their lives backed up their message. Just as the Lord Jesus Christ made a difference in their lives, He wants to make a difference in our lives today. So, what about you? Is your life backing up your testimony? What I'm saying is that a life of faithfulness will produce a life worth emulating. A life of faithfulness is a life worth following. This is why our text goes on to say, "Imitate their faith." Look at it one more time: "Remember your leaders who spoke the word of God to you. Consider the outcome of their way of life and imitate their faith" (Hebrews 13:7).

The word *Imitate* comes from a Greek word from which we get our words *mimic* and *mime*. It can also be interpreted as "an actor" in the good sense of the word. We are to look to the lives of those who have gone before us and mimic their faith, or act like them! In other words, we can make a difference with our lives today if we will allow the Lord to work through us, if we will look at the faithfulness of those who have gone before us and imitate, or mimic, their faith. This is why Paul says in 1 Corinthians 4:16, "Therefore I urge you to imitate me."

He also says in 1 Thessalonians 1:6, "You became imitators of us and of the Lord."

Paul didn't say these things because he was terribly conceited and full of himself. He said these things because he was doing his best to live for Christ and model for others what it meant to be a Christian.

Now let me ask you, who is the Christian you would most want to be like? I don't mean Franklin Graham or Max Lucado or someone else who's famous. I mean who is the Christian you are personally acquainted with that you would most want to be like? Are you thinking of someone? Now let me encourage you to do this: get to know them, spend time with them, and ask them what they do to grow in their spiritual lives. This Christian you admire so much came to know the Lord the same way you came to know the Lord—by putting their faith and trust in Jesus Christ.

The verb translated *imitate* is used in the continuous sense, suggesting this should be a constant habit or practice. In other words, we are to make a habit of following the godly faith of our forefathers. In addition, we are to actively look for role models and follow their examples. We are to mentor and be mentored in the Christian life.

In Titus chapter 2, Paul is talking specifically to older men and women, and he encourages them to set godly examples for the younger Christians following along behind. Specifically, he says,

> In everything set them an example by doing what is good. In your teaching show integrity, seriousness and soundness of speech that cannot be condemned, so that those who oppose you may be ashamed because they have nothing bad to say about us (Titus 2:7).

As Christians, we all start at the same place, and then the growth is up to us. Of course, God does His part, but it's up to us to pray, read our Bibles, attend church, meditate on scripture, tell others about Christ, and so on. When we have an eternal perspective on life, we will be able to see what is really important, and we will spend our time doing those things. In Ephesians 5:1–2, the Bible challenges us with, "Be imitators of God, therefore, as dearly loved children and live a life of love, just as Christ loved us and gave himself up for us as a fragrant offering and sacrifice to God."

The word *imitators* in this passage is the same word we find in Hebrews 13:7. We are to make it a habit to try to imitate God in our lives. In other words, you can be like that person you admire so much, because you have access to the same God.

However, far too many Christians not only look to the past, but also try to live in the past. They longingly talk about how things used to be in their current church, or some previous church, instead of making a difference where they are right now. The same Jesus who helped us in the past wants to make a difference in our lives today! Listen, be proud of all your yesterdays, but remember that today is the yesterday of tomorrow. What are you doing with your life today that is making a difference for Jesus Christ? God wants every day of our lives to count for Him. Our relationship with the Lord is more than just a fond memory of the past. This is why I say, "Look to the past, but live in the present, as we long for the future."

Our future is bright for us as believers. We have hope for the future based upon what Christ has done for us in the past. I am thoroughly convinced that our brightest days are still ahead of us. I mean, after all, it rained for forty days and forty nights before Noah could stick his head out of the ark. Abraham was seventy-five before God called him out of Ur. The children of Israel wandered for forty years in the wilderness before they were able to enter the Promised Land. Jesus lived for thirty years before He started his earthly ministry. We have only just begun to accomplish all the Lord has for us in this life.

This emphasis upon the future does not diminish anything the Lord has done in the past. On the contrary, we praise God for what has happened in the past, but we look to the future with eagerness and anticipation. We eagerly look to the future, because we know the same Jesus who helped us in the past is ready, willing, and able to do even greater things as we work together toward the future.

I came across a great quote on this subject. Kenneth C. Haugk, writing in *Antagonists in the Church,* says,

> God's church is constantly on the move, bravely following the Master. The Good Shepherd knows sheep: fresh pastures are a requirement. Left too long to work over the same pasture, sheep crop the grass to the roots and kill it. God keeps his flock on the move to supply fresh, green pastures watered by deep streams. So, putting aside what lies behind and reaching toward what lies ahead, your congregation can be strengthened, growing into the fullness that God intends.[21]

It was never God's intention for anyone to stay the same. People grow. People change. People adapt to their surroundings. The same is true for the church. Our message will never change, but our methods have to change if we are going to reach those God has placed in our mission field. If we stay in one place too long, the sheep become restless, the field becomes sparse, and the pasture begins to stink. But if we will let Him, God will lead us to fresh pastures, to new fields, and to fresh water. However, we have to be obedient to follow.

I came across an illustration from the life of Babe Ruth that emphasizes what I'm trying to communicate in this chapter. Babe Ruth reportedly once said, "Most people who really counted in my life were never famous. Nobody ever heard of them, except those who knew them and loved them. I especially recall an old minister I once knew ... I have written my name on thousands of baseballs in my life. The old minister wrote his name on just a few simple hearts, but how I envy him. He was not trying to please himself. Fame never came his way. I am listed as a home run hitter, yet beside this minister ... I have never gotten to first base."

---

[21] Kenneth C. Haugk, *Antagonists in the Church: How to Identify and Deal with Destructive Conflict* (Minneapolis: Augsburg Press, 1988), p. 183.

Babe Ruth apparently grew to understand that truly great people in life are not necessarily the rich and famous. The truly great people are the ones who do things to make their lives count for all eternity. My guess is the majority of those reading this book came to Christ because of the efforts of someone most people have never heard of. It was a faithful Sunday school teacher, a faithful deacon or deacon's wife, a faithful pastor, or a faithful neighbor who picked you up and took you to church, or maybe a relative or coworker who loved you into the kingdom.

The author of Hebrews is challenging us on several levels to remember those who have made an impact on our lives, but do not stop there. Remember the past, but live in the present, as you long for the future. In other words, do something worthy of imitation with your life. Be the person of whom someone says, "He impacted my life for Christ." Be the person of whom someone says, "She brought me to Jesus." Be the person of whom someone says, "I once knew a lady who was facing all kinds of struggles and difficulties, but she was such a godly example to me." Live a life worthy of imitation, because the same Jesus who helped us in the past is ready to help us today, and He wants to help us in the future! A few years ago, Christian recording artist, Steve Green, recorded a very popular song entitled, "Find Us Faithful." I want to challenge you with a portion of the lyrics from this song:

> After all our hopes and dreams have come and gone
> And our children sift through all we've left behind
> May the clues that they discover
> And the memories they uncover
> Become the light that leads them
> To the road we each must find
> Oh may all who come behind us find us faithful
> Oh may all who come behind us find us faithful[22]

---

[22] Steve Green (1988), "Find Us Faithful," Birdwing Music/Jonathan Mark Music (admin. by The Sparrow Corp.) Retrieved from www.stevegreenministries.org/product/find-us-faithful-7/

This is my prayer for each one of us today. May all who come behind us find us faithful because we lived a life worthy of imitation. Tim Kimmel, the author I quoted back at the beginning of this chapter, says he keeps six photos on his desk. The one on the left is a photo of the hospital where he was born. The one on the right is a photo of the cemetery where all of his relatives are buried. And the photos in the center are of his wife and children. Writing about these photos, he says, "Don't forget, Tim, this is where you checked in, this is where you're checking out, and the four people in the middle are why you are here."[23]

Here is a man with an eternal perspective—he is thanking God for those who have gone before him and taking responsibility for those coming along behind. I pray God would help us to do the same. This focus upon an eternal perspective leads directly to chapter 8, which emphasizes finishing well.

---

[23] Tim Kimmel, *Little House on the Freeway: Help for the Hurried Home* (Colorado Springs: Multnomah Books, 1987), p. 168.

MARK S. MILWEE

CHAPTER EIGHT

‗‗

Finishing Well

I recently came across the following anecdotes about aging. The first is a story told about Jeanne Calment, who at the time of the story was the oldest living person whose age could be verified. On her 120th birthday, she was asked to describe her vision of the future. She replied, "Very brief!" Another woman was asked the benefits of living to the age of 102. After a short pause, she said, "Well, there's not a lot of peer pressure!" John Fetterman of Grace Episcopal Church in Madison, Wisconsin, tells of an elderly woman in his congregation who died, and since she was never married, she had requested there be no pallbearers at her funeral. In her final instructions she wrote, "They wouldn't take me out while I was alive, and I don't want them to take me out when I'm dead!"

I believe it's not how you start, but how you finish, that counts in your Christian life. There is something to be said for finishing well. I've observed dozens of people over the years start strong but later fall by the wayside. There is no greater testimony than a life of faithful consistency. This is what I mean by finishing well. Finishing well is the ability to keep striving, keep working, and keep pressing on in your Christian life. It is taking up your cross daily year after year after year, and doing your best to serve and obey the Lord. This idea reminds me of a familiar quote from Teddy Roosevelt. I'm sure you have heard it at some point along the way, but it is worth repeating. He states,

> It is not the critic who counts, not the man who points out how the strong man stumbles, or where the doer of deeds could have done them better. The credit belongs to the man in the arena, whose face is marred by dust and sweat and blood, who strives valiantly ... who knows the great enthusiasms, the great devotions, who spends himself in a worthy cause, who at the best knows in the end the triumph of high achievement, and who at the worst, if he fails, at least fails while daring greatly, so that his place shall never be with those cold and timid souls who have never known neither victory nor defeat.[24]

So with this in mind, I would like to propose in this chapter that finishing well requires that we remember several important principles. The first principle of finishing well is to remember where you have been. Titus 3:3 says,

> For we ourselves were once foolish, disobedient, led astray, slaves to various passions and pleasures, passing our days in malice and envy, hated by others and hating one another.

As I said above, the first principle of finishing well is to remember where you've been. In other words, remember what it was that God

---

[24] Theodore Roosevelt, "The Man in the Arena," speech given by former President of the United States Theodore Roosevelt at the Sorbonne in Paris, France, on April 23, 1910. Retrieved from http://www.theodore-roosevelt. com/images/research/speeches/maninthearena.pdf (15 April 2018).

saved you from. Verse 3 begins, "For we ourselves were once ..." (Titus 3:3a). You might want to circle or underline "we ourselves" in your Bible. We need to be reminded of the pit the Lord pulled us out from. Again, it's good for us to consider how we were living before we came to Christ, and maybe this will help us be more patient with those we are trying to reach today.

Paul is describing the conditions in his day, but things are no better today. He says that before we were saved, we were foolish, disobedient, and led astray. In other words, we were deceived. He then goes on to say we were slaves to various passions and pleasures. We lived in malice and envy. In other words, we were consumed by our passions and lust. We wanted bad things to happen to others. We were jealous of their possessions, skills, talents, and abilities. The end result was that we hated each other.

I understand some of you reading this just nod your head and say, "Yes, this pretty accurately describes my life before Christ." However, others might think, *This doesn't describe my life at all. I don't remember hating anyone, or being jealous of anyone, or trying to hurt anyone.* Well, praise God, but this is a description of what the world is like without Christ. It's a desperate picture, but I think you will agree this also truthfully portrays the world in which we live.

Every day we are bombarded by death, misery, and injustice. We live in a fallen, sin-sick world, a sinful world whose only hope is Jesus Christ. If you have not experienced many of these things, then rejoice in your good fortune! But also understand that this is the reality many people find themselves in today. Remembering what God saved us from helps us to appreciate what God has done for us, and it also helps us appreciate what God is trying to do for others. The first principle, then, of finishing well is to remember where you've been.

The second principle of finishing well is to remember when you changed. Look at Titus 3, beginning with verse 4:

But when the goodness and loving kindness of God our Savior appeared, he saved us, not because of works done by us in righteousness, but according to his own mercy, by the washing of regeneration and renewal of the Holy Spirit, whom he poured out on us richly through Jesus Christ our Savior (Titus 3:4–6).

Carefully examine the beginning of verse 5. It declares, "He saved us!" When I was growing up in small country churches in the Bible Belt, there was a song we would often sing, especially during revivals. It was a catchy little tune, and it goes like this: "It was on a Monday somebody touched me ..." We would sing through every day of the week, and the fun part of the song was, on your day—whatever day it happened to be when you were saved—when we got to your day, you would get to stand up. But we were also very accommodating; just so that no one got their feelings hurt or felt left out, we would sing the last verse. It goes like this: "I don't know what day it was, but somebody touched me!"

Now, I've got to admit, I never could understand the folks who stood up on the last verse. How could they not know what day it was? As the years have passed, I've come to understand that days and dates are sometimes hard to remember. But I do believe we should all remember a time when we put our faith and trust in the Lord Jesus Christ.

Basically, this passage is teaching us how God took the initiative in saving us. God provided the way of salvation. Jesus Christ came to make this salvation available to us. The emphasis is not so much on *when* as it is on *what*. What Christ has done for us, He did not force into our lives. He comes in response to our invitation. The Bible says that in order to be saved, you have to confess with your mouth, "Jesus is Lord, and I believe in my heart that God has raised him from the dead." He stands at the door and knocks, but we open the door and let Him in.

So, let me ask you a question: Are you sure you've invited Him in? He's provided a way for salvation, but can you remember a time in your life when you prayed and invited Jesus Christ to come in and be the Lord of your life? I ask this question because in order to finish well, we need to have matters settled with God. We should be remembering not only where we've been, but also when we changed.

The third principle of finishing well is to remember whose you are. Have you ever heard someone say, "Well, I always try to do the right thing, and hopefully when I die, my good deeds will outweigh the bad"? It is like God is sitting in heaven with a giant scale, and our life is hanging in the balance. On one side, He places or takes into consideration all of our good deeds, all of our acts of kindness, and on the other side He places all of our bad deeds or bad decisions … and if we are lucky, the first side will outweigh the second side. Have you ever heard anyone talk like this? I've heard even Christians talk this way! Please listen carefully; what I've just described is not a biblical teaching! It doesn't matter how many good things you do. You can spend your life doing good things and still miss out on heaven. Just being good has never saved anyone. Look at what the Bible says in Titus 3, beginning with verse 5:

> He saved us, not because of righteous things we
> have done, but because of his mercy. He saved us
> through the washing of rebirth and renewal by the
> Holy Spirit, whom he poured out on us generously
> through Jesus Christ our Savior" (Titus 3:5–6).

Someone said it this way: "Salvation is the root. Good works are the fruit." Good works are not the way to salvation. Good works are the result of salvation. The bottom line is, no matter how hard you try, you cannot save yourself. It's not "who" you are but "whose" you are that makes all the difference. How do I know? Well, verse 5 illustrates this truth as well as any passage in the Bible. There is a strong contrast in verse 5. The contrast is between our works and

God's mercy. The verse says, "He saved *us, not* because of righteous things we have done, *but* because of *his* mercy." (Titus 3:5a; italics mine).

Notice the words *not* and *us* in the first half of the verse and *but* and *his* in the latter half of the verse. There is a double emphasis in both halves of the verse strongly emphasizing that God's mercy saves us, not our own efforts to save ourselves. You cannot save yourself! You just can't do it! This is so important to understand, because so many people in our world today believe if they can just stay out of trouble, keep their noses clean, do the right thing, and live a morally good life, then everything is going to be okay. But this is not what the Bible teaches.

Take, for example, the case of the rich young ruler. Here was a young man who lived an impeccable life. The Bible says he had obeyed all of the commandments since he was a child. He came to Jesus eager to follow, but the Bible says he went away sorrowful, because Jesus knew his heart, and Jesus asked him to give something up he just couldn't let go of. He wanted to come to God on his own terms, but we all have to come to God on God's terms. God doesn't conform to us. We conform to Him! Oh, but why wouldn't we, when we fully understand what is being offered to us? Look back at the remainder of verse 5 and then at verse 6: "He saved us through the washing of rebirth and renewal by the Holy Spirit, whom he poured out on us generously through Jesus Christ our Savior" (Titus 3:5b–6).

Notice, first, all three persons of the Trinity are present in the salvation process: God saved us through the washing of rebirth and renewal by the Holy Spirit, whom He (God) poured out on us generously through Jesus Christ, our Savior. At the moment you are saved, God unleashes the power of the Holy Spirit in your life because of what Christ has done for you. You are washed and cleansed into rebirth. This is illustrative of your new life in Christ. This is why Paul says in 2 Corinthians, "Therefore, if anyone is in

Christ, he is a new creation. The old has passed away; behold, the new has come" (2 Corinthians 5:17).

You are reborn in Christ. Jesus said to Nicodemus, "You must be born again." (John 3:7b) So, there's the moment of salvation (regeneration), but there is also renewal, which is an ongoing process. The same word for renewal is used in Romans 12:2:

> Do not be conformed to this world, but be transformed by the renewal of your mind, that by testing you may discern what is the will of God, what is good and acceptable and perfect.

The idea is of an ongoing, continual process of renewal in your life through your personal relationship with Jesus Christ. So, remember it's not who you are, but whose you are that counts in God's kingdom. You cannot save yourself. The entire Trinity has done the work for you, if you will follow the Lord in obedience. The third principle of finishing well is to remember whose you are.

The fourth and final principle of finishing well is to remember where you are going. Look at Titus 3:7–8:

> So that being justified by his grace we might become heirs according to the hope of eternal life. The saying is trustworthy, and I want you to insist on these things, so that those who have believed in God may be careful to devote themselves to good works. These things are excellent and profitable for people.

Now I'm going to share something remarkable with you, so I want you to pay close attention. No matter what you have done in this life, you are still eligible to receive God's grace. A number of years ago, the church where I was the pastor began airing our worship service on the local community access cable channel. This was south of San Jose in the San Francisco Bay Area, and the local cable was broadcast into over two hundred thousand homes. At least, this many people had access to it. Not long after we started doing this, people began calling our church and asking for appointments to meet with me.

One afternoon, I met with a beautiful young lady who told me she couldn't come to our church, because if she stepped inside the building, the roof would fall in. She went on to share with me how she had spent her young life as a prostitute, and how she was sure God could never save her. I had the joy of explaining to her how God's grace was sufficient even for her. She then prayed with me to receive Jesus Christ as her personal Lord and Savior!

Grace is God's undeserved gift to us, and to be justified means to be made right. My favorite definition of justification says justification means that it is just-as-if-I had never sinned! When we trust Christ in faith, we are made right with God through the undeserved gift of God's grace. We have to go back to verse 3 and remember that at one time we too were separated from God because of our sin. But God, through His grace and mercy, saw fit to save us. As a result of this salvation, we have become heirs, heirs of the promise of eternal life!

We are heirs of the promise, and therefore we hold onto the hope of eternal life. I've done more than my share of funerals since I became a pastor. I've done so many, I've practically memorized all of the passages I like to share at memorial services, but one passage I never tire of hearing talks about the hope we have in Christ. It is found in 1 Thessalonians 4 beginning with verse 13:

> But we do not want you to be uninformed, brothers, about those who are asleep, that you may not grieve as others do who have no hope. For since we believe that Jesus died and rose again, even so, through Jesus, God will bring with him those who have fallen asleep. For this we declare to you by a word from the Lord, that we who are alive, who are left

until the coming of the Lord, will not precede those who have fallen asleep. For the Lord himself will descend from heaven with a cry of command, with the voice of an archangel, and with the sound of the trumpet of God. And the dead in Christ will rise first. Then we who are alive, who are left, will be caught up together with them in the clouds to meet the Lord in the air, and so we will always be with the Lord. Therefore encourage one another with these words (1 Thessalonians 4:13–18).

Paul says he is sharing these words so we will not grieve as those who have no hope. We have hope because we know where we are going. We have hope because our salvation is secure. We have hope because we know in whom we have believed, and we know that He is able to keep what has been promised. This is why we can encourage each other with these words. It's not that we are rejoicing in death. We miss our friends and loved ones terribly. We didn't want them to leave us, but we have hope in Christ that we will see them again. This is the hope of eternal life for all who have put their faith and trust in the Lord Jesus Christ.

So the process of finishing well begins by remembering what we were saved from. It continues by being reminded of when we changed. It concludes as we remember where we are going and diligently serve until God takes us home to be with Him. I believe the greatest motivational factor for finishing well—for not giving up, for not losing hope, for continuing to strive even when the road gets tough and difficult—is to remember where you are going. John reminds us in 1 John 5:13: "I write these things to you who believe in the name of the Son of God that you may know that you have eternal life."

Therefore, we can approach the twilight years of our lives with confidence, knowing we have a better home waiting for us just over on the other side. The implication is that people are watching our lives, and if we are careful to devote ourselves to the teachings of Christ, others will want to follow our example. We are all called upon to finish well, because a life of faithful consistency is a lasting testimony for Christ. Let me put it this way: there is an inscription at the Chester Cathedral entitled "Time's Paces," and it simply says,

> When as a child, I roamed at will, time stood still.
> When as a youth, I laughed and talked, time walked.
> When at last I became a man, time ran.
> Then as I older grew, time flew.
> Soon I will find while passing on, time gone.

We are given only a certain amount of time on this earth to live a life of faithful consistency for the Lord. I can think of no greater testimony than for someone to say on the day of my death, "He finished well!"

CHAPTER NINE

"Are You Afraid to Die?"

A number of years ago while I was serving a church in Fremont, California, I would often get calls from the local funeral home asking if I could help with services. There were only four mortuaries in this city of over two hundred thousand people, and many of the folks did not have a church home. Our church was really close by, and as a result, I got to know the staff at the local funeral home very well.

I was helping with one of these services one afternoon, and following the service at the mortuary, I was riding in a hearse with the undertaker to the graveside ceremony. We passed the local hospital, and I asked my friend Jeff, the undertaker, "What happens when someone dies at the hospital? Is there a room where they take the people, or do you have to go up to the hospital room to get them? How does that work?" He told me about the procedure they follow and the appropriate protocol. Then I said, "Well, I was just wondering, because in my volunteer work as a chaplain at the hospital, I've been in the room many times when someone has died."

Now, remember, we were riding in a hearse with a dead body right behind us, and he turned and looked over at me in the passenger seat of the hearse and exclaimed, "You've been in the room when someone has died?"

"Well, yeah," I answered.

He responded, "Man, that's creepy!"

How do you respond to an undertaker who says your job is creepy?

I vividly remember one particular day at the hospital, because of the stark contrast between the individuals I went to see. As a volunteer chaplain, I was often called to visit with people I had never met before. So, I was called to the hospital one day to visit with two different ladies, both of whom were very near to death. I did not know their spiritual condition. I had never met these ladies before, but I do know one seemed to have a sense of calm and peace, while the other was wild-eyed and appeared to be very frantic and upset. She was thrashing about on the bed and couldn't seem to relax. I could definitely be wrong, and I'm certainly not the Holy Spirit, but it seemed very clear to me that one lady was prepared to die, while the other was not. I'll never forget the stark contrast between what I encountered in the different rooms.

I believe the research of Dr. Maurice Rawlings, a man who has done extensive research with near-death experiences, can shed some light on my experiences that day. He reports that half of the people he interviewed following near-death experiences have a vision of hell rather than a vision of heaven. Ironically, we don't ever hear about these experiences. All we ever hear about is some kind of bright light that draws you lovingly to itself. But apparently, according to Dr. Rawlings, half of the people who have these types of experiences have seen something quite different.

Now, why would one person facing death have a sense of calm, peace, and tranquility, while the other is frantic, panicked, and filled with fear? Why would one person have a vision of heaven and the other a vision of hell? I believe the answer is found in a personal relationship with Jesus Christ. It seems obvious to me. Christians can face death with the calm assurance that everything's going to be all right. The Lord has prepared a place for us. He is going to wipe away every tear from our eyes. We are entering into the rest He has promised. But for non-Christians death brings horror. They are crossing over into an eternity separated from God—an eternity of pain and misery … an eternity banished from God's presence and ushered into the presence of Satan and his demons.

If you've ever seen the movie *Ghost*, you might remember the scene where the evil person dies and the black ghouls come to take the person away. I vividly remember the ear-piercing screams, which made me squirm in my seat, and the sight of black demons coming up out of the earth and taking this man away. I remember because it frightened me very much. Now, I certainly don't recommend building your theology on what we see in the movies, but I was glad to see the portrayal of the consequences of an evil life as depicted in this film.

I once called a local funeral home and tried to convince them to loan me a casket to use as a backdrop for a sermon I was planning on death, but I couldn't talk them into it. However, when I told the lady at the funeral home why I wanted the casket, she said something I thought was very profound. She said, "Some people are so afraid of dying that they forget to live!"

So, let me ask you a question: Are you afraid of dying? Of course, Satan will try to convince you that you have nothing to worry about. He will try to deceive you and tell you that you've got plenty of time. Hell is going to just be one big party. But don't believe it. I believe in a literal hell, and hell is a horrible place! Hell is described in the Bible as a place of weeping and gnashing of teeth, a place where the worm does not die, a terrible and horrific place where you do not want to go, where you do not want a loved one to go, a place where you do not want anyone you even remotely care about to go.

There is a great deal of interest these days in the afterlife and what happens when we die. Randy Alcorn's book *Heaven* has been very popular; or maybe you've read the fascinating book by Erwin Lutzer titled, *One Minute after You Die*. I found both of these books to be quite intriguing, but questions about death and what happens when we die are as old as life itself. In the book of Job, which many believe to be one of the oldest books in the Bible, Job asks a thought-provoking question (Job 14:14): "If a man dies, shall he live again?"

This is a good question. What do you think? If a man dies, will he live again? In other words, what is the appropriate Christian response to death? Paul addresses this topic in 1 Corinthians 15 by asking two key questions:

1. "O, Death, where is your victory?"
2. "O, Death, where is your sting?"

Let's start with the second question first: "O, Death, where is your sting?"

(1 Corinthians 15:55b). Paul answers his own question by saying, "The sting of death is sin." Why did he choose these words? *Sting* is a strong word. If you have ever experienced any type of insect sting, you know the power behind this word, but what Paul is describing here is much more powerful than a bee sting. The "sting" Paul is referring to is the feelings of helplessness a non-Christian will experience at the moment of death. The sting of death is the helpless feeling you experience as you sit in the hospital room of a loved one who is slipping away without the Lord. You know deep down in your heart Jesus Christ is their only hope, but they refuse to listen to you. The sting of death is the sin that separates us from a holy God. I believe the moment, the instant, the second a non-Christian dies, the realization hits them immediately that they are lost for all eternity, separated from God.

So, maybe you are wondering, what actually happens to a nonbeliever when they die without Christ? Do goons come to get you and drag you away screaming into hell? I can't tell you exactly how it all happens, but Jesus once shared a story about a man who died without God. Let's see what happened to him. The story is recorded in Luke 16 beginning with verse 19.

There was a rich man who was clothed in purple and fine linen and who feasted sumptuously every day. And at his gate was laid a poor man named Lazarus, covered with sores, who desired to be fed with what fell from the rich man's table. Moreover, even the dogs came and licked his sores. The poor man died and was carried by the angels to Abraham's side. The rich man also died and was buried, and in Hades, being in torment, he lifted up his eyes and saw Abraham far off and Lazarus at his side. And he called out, "Father Abraham, have mercy on me, and send Lazarus to dip the end of his finger in water and cool my tongue, for I am in anguish in this flame." But Abraham said, "Child, remember that you in your lifetime received your good things, and Lazarus in like manner bad things; but now he is comforted here, and you are in anguish. And besides all this, between us and you a great chasm has been fixed, in order that those who would pass from here to you may not be able, and none may cross from there to us." And he said, "Then I beg you, father, to send him to my father's house—for I have five brothers—so that he may warn them, lest they also come into this place of torment." But Abraham said, "They have Moses and the Prophets; let them hear them." And he said, "No, father Abraham, but if someone goes to them from the dead, they will repent." He said to him, "If they do not hear Moses and the Prophets, neither will they be convinced if someone should rise from the dead" (Luke 16:19–31).

I would like to point out a few truths from this passage about death and the nonbeliever. First, hell is a real place of pain and torment. Verse 22 ends by saying, "The rich man also died and was buried" (Luke 16:22b).

Now, read verse 23: "And in Hades, being in torment, he lifted up his eyes and saw Abraham far off and Lazarus at his side" (Luke 16:23).

Some people do not believe hell and hades are the same place; still others do not believe in hell at all. They say hell is just a figment of our imaginations as Christians; but try to tell this to the rich man in torment. You can call it hades if you want and say it is not really hell, but the Bible clearly says this man was in torment. You can say hell is just the product of an overactive Christian imagination, but the sting of death for you will be the stark reality of an eternity spent in a literal hell once you die without Christ. The Bible says you will be eternally separated from God and banished forever to a place of torment and torture. This is not just my opinion—this is what the Bible teaches. The Bible says hell is a place of torment both physically and mentally. The rich man could actually see Abraham far away and Lazarus by his side. This could possibly be one of the worst aspects of hell—being able to see what you are missing. Look back with me at verse 25: "But Abraham said, 'Child, remember that you in your lifetime received your good things, and Lazarus in like manner bad things; but now he is comforted here, and you are in anguish'" (Luke 16:25).

This verse implies you will be able to remember in hell all of the things you did or did not do while here on earth. You will be able to remember all of the opportunities you ever had to accept the gospel. These events will continually replay in your mind—this is the mental torture of hell. But the mental torture is nothing to compare with the physical tortures. Notice verse 24: "And he called out, 'Father Abraham, have mercy on me, and send Lazarus to dip the end of his finger in water and cool my tongue, for I am in anguish in this flame'" (Luke 16:24).

A recent *U.S. News & World Report* poll revealed that 64 percent of Americans believe there is a hell; 25 percent say there isn't a hell;

and 9 percent don't know. Most respondents think of hell as "an anguished state of existence" or "an unpleasant solitary confinement" rather than as a real place. Professor Douglas Groothius of Denver Seminary believes many Christians are ashamed of the doctrine of hell, but Tim Keller, pastor of Redeemer Presbyterian Church in New York City, worries about downplaying the reality of hell. He believes that doing this "does irreparable damage to our deepest comforts—our understanding of God's grace and love … To preach the good news, we must preach the bad."

So, what do you think? Can the threat of spending eternity in hell motivate individuals toward faith and virtue? Professor Jerry L. Walls of Asbury Theological Seminary, writing in *Christianity Today,* believes, "If there is no God, no heaven, no hell, there simply is no persuasive reason to be moral." In other words, "Why live a moral life if there are no consequences for immorality?"

Charlie Peace, a condemned criminal in England, on the day he was being taken to his execution, listened to a minister reading from the word of God. And when he found out he was reading about heaven and hell, he looked at the preacher and said, "Sir, if I believed what you and the church of God say, and even if England were covered with broken glass from coast to coast, I would walk over it on hands and knees and think it worthwhile living just to save one soul from an eternal hell like that."[25]

Hell is a real place you want to avoid at all costs. Hell is not a place you ever want any of your friends or loved ones to go. The rich man begs Abraham to send someone to warn his brothers before they also end up in this place of torture. The sting of death for nonbelievers is an eternity separated from God in hell because of our sin.

Paul gives a second answer to his question, "O, death, where is your sting?" He says, "The power of sin is the law." (1 Corinthians

---

[25] Charlie Peace, quoted in James Emory White, *Serious Times: Making Your Life Matter in an Urgent Day* (Downers Grove, Illinois: Intervarsity Press, 2004), p. 161.

15:56b) What law is he talking about? He could have been referring to the Covenant Law given to the children of Israel through Moses, including the Ten Commandments. He could have been referring to the words of Christ during the Sermon on the Mount. But more specifically, I believe he is referring to the law of sin. The law of sin is this: sin leads to death, which leads to eternal separation from God in hell. It goes like this:

> For all have sinned and fall short of the glory of God (Romans 3:23).

> The wages of sin is death (Romans 6:23).

> And just as it is appointed for man to die once, and after that comes judgment (Hebrews 9:27).

> And if anyone's name was not found written in the book of life, he was thrown into the lake of fire (Revelation 20:15).

Although no one seems to want to talk about it anymore, and even more don't want to believe it, the Bible is very clear: a life of disobedience to God leads to spiritual death, which leads to judgment, which leads to an eternity separated from God in hell. This is the law of sin, and it is the sting of death to the nonbeliever. Now, this would be a very sad chapter if it ended now, but we have two questions to deal with, and thus far we've looked at only one. We've examined the sting of death, but now let's turn our attention to the second question: "O, death, where is your victory?" This question is found in 1 Corinthians 15:55a: "O, Death, where is your victory?"

Death has no victory over the Christian. In verse 54 of this same passage Paul tells us for the Christian, death is swallowed up in victory. Verse 57 describes the source of this victory: "But thanks be to God, who gives us the victory through our Lord Jesus Christ" (1 Corinthians 15:57).

Our victory comes from knowing Jesus Christ as our personal Lord and Savior. One of my favorite stories to share at memorial services is about a family out taking a ride in the country on a warm summer day. They have all of the windows in the car down and are enjoying the breeze, when out of nowhere a bee flies into the window, and the little girl in the backseat begins to scream. She is screaming frantically, because she is terribly allergic to bee stings. Her father gently pulls the car over to the side of the road, and he reaches back into the backseat and traps the bee with his hand. He holds it there for just a moment and then releases his hand. The bee starts flying around again, and the girl starts screaming again, but the father says, "No, no, honey, look!" She looks, and embedded there in her father's hand is the stinger from the bee. He allowed the bee to sting him so his little girl would be safe. In other words, he took the sting so his daughter would not have to.

This is precisely what Christ has done for us. He has taken the sting of death upon himself, so that we can find victory over death. He is saying to us, "No, no, look! Look at my hands. Look at my side. Look at my feet. Stop doubting and believe." This is why Paul writes, "But thanks be to God, who gives us the victory through our Lord Jesus Christ!" Death has no victory over the Christian. Death has no sting for those who are in Christ. Death has been swallowed up in victory because of what Jesus Christ has done for us. Our victory comes through our personal relationship with Him.

Earlier, I shared with you the familiar verse found in Romans 6:23, but I deliberately shared only the first half of the verse: "For the wages of sin is death …" Now we are ready for the remainder of the verse: "But the free gift of God is eternal life through Jesus Christ our Lord." I've spent a great deal of time in this chapter warning you about the realities of a literal hell, but the good news is that you do not have to go there. You can spend an eternity in heaven with Christ, but the choice is up to you. I often quote the following comforting words from Jesus at memorial services. They are found in John 14:1–6. In these verses, we find assurance when Christ says He has prepared a place for us in heaven and we will one day be with Him. In these verses Jesus says to us,

> "Let not your hearts be troubled. Believe in God; believe also in me. In my Father's house are many rooms. If it were not so, would I have told you that I go to prepare a place for you? And if I go and prepare a place for you, I will come again and will take you to myself, that where I am you may be also. And you know the way to where I am going." Thomas said to him, "Lord, we do not know where you are going. How can we know the way?" Jesus said to him, "I am the way, and the truth, and the life. No one comes to the Father except through me" (John 14:1–6).

There are all kinds of ways to prepare to die, but only one way that really counts. Michael Landon Jr. once said after learning that he was terminally ill,

> While life lasts, it's good to remember that death is coming, and it's good we don't know when. It keeps us alert, reminds us to live while we have the chance. Somebody should tell us right at the start of our lives that we are dying. There are only so many tomorrows.[26]

I heard about a conversation a man overheard on a ham radio. I can't remember the entire conversation, but the gist of it was that

---

[26] Michael Landon Jr., "Goodreads Quote," accessed 26 July 2009, https://www.goodreads.com
/quotes/228182-somebody-should-tell-us-right-at-the-start-of-our.

an older man was talking to a younger man, and he told him he had figured out how many Saturdays we have in our lifetime. He calculated this out, and then he put marbles in a jar representing how many he calculated that he had left. He then took one out each Saturday so he could see the number diminish. He said it helped him to realize what is really important in life, and to not waste his time doing things that did not matter.

He then said to his younger friend, "I just took the last one out this morning. So I figure I'm living on borrowed time, but I'm going to make the most of the time I have left!" Death is no respecter of persons. Every day thousands of people die from all walks of life. Some are cut down in the prime of their lives, while others live long, full lives, but one thing is certain: unless the Lord comes back first, we are all going to die.

The date of one's death is a mystery—no one knows the day or the hour when his or her time will come. This is why it's imperative for us to get ready, that we take care of business, before it's eternally too late. If you are counting on a deathbed conversion, if you are saying to yourself, "I'll just live any way I want to live. I'll do whatever I please. I'll just make things right before I die," let me tell you from personal experience—you might not get that chance.

I've been in rooms with several people who were so drugged and hooked up to all kinds of machines that they couldn't have prayed if they had wanted to. They were not even conscious of what was going on around them. I read about when Princess Diana had her tragic car accident. Her last words were, "Leave me alone." She was in so much pain that she didn't want anyone near her.

You're not guaranteed the time or the mental capacity to be saved just before you die. This is why you need to think about your eternal destiny today, and while you're thinking about it, think about this: God wants you to spend eternity in heaven with Him. Jesus prayed, "Father, I desire that they also, whom you have given me, may be with me where I am, to see my glory that you have given me because you loved me before the foundation of the world."

(John 17:24) If you believe in the Lord Jesus Christ, you don't have to be afraid of death. Jesus said to the thief on the cross who put his faith in him, "Today you will be with me in paradise" (Luke 23:43). The apostle Paul said, "My desire is to depart and be with Christ" (Philippians1:23).

Heaven is a wonderful place. Listen to this description from the book of Revelation:

> And I saw the holy city, new Jerusalem, coming down out of heaven from God, prepared as a bride adorned for her husband. And I heard a loud voice from the throne saying, "Behold, the dwelling place of God is with man. He will dwell with them, and they will be his people, and God himself will be with them as their God. He will wipe away every tear from their eyes, and death shall be no more, neither shall there be mourning, nor crying, nor pain anymore, for the former things have passed away. And he who was seated on the throne said, "Behold, I am making all things new." Also he said, "Write this down, for these words are trustworthy and true" (Revelation 21:2–5).

D. L. Moody, the famous evangelist, once said, "It's not the jeweled walls and pearly gates that are going to make heaven attractive. It is being with God." We are going to be in heaven with God.

So, how will you react when death comes calling? I heard that when Thomas Paine wrote the book *The Age of Reason,* he wrote it with the intention of undermining Christianity. However, on his deathbed, he reportedly cried out,

> I would give worlds, if I had them, that *The Age of Reason* had not been published. Oh, Lord, Help

Me! Christ, help me! Oh God, what have I done to suffer so much? But there is no God! If there should be, what will become of me now? Stay with me, for God's sake. Send even a child to stay with me for it is hell to be alone. If ever the devil had an agent, I have been that one.[27]

Here are the tortured, confused ramblings of a man calling out, on his deathbed, to the God he had always said he didn't believe in.

Voltaire, a French agnostic, who also wrote against Christianity, is said to have screamed on his deathbed, "I am abandoned by God and man! I will give you half of what I am worth, if you will give me six months of life … Oh Christ! Oh, Jesus Christ!"[28] A nurse who attended him in his final hours reportedly said, "For all the wealth in Europe, I would not see another nonbeliever die."

Now, compare these tragic deaths scenes to the final words of a few notable Christians:

"I see earth receding, and heaven is opening. God is calling me"[29] (Dwight L. Moody).

"The best of all is, God is with us. Farewell. Farewell"[30] (John Wesley).

"Speak less of Dr. Carey and more of Dr. Carey's Savior" (William Carey).

"I have pain; but I have peace. I have peace" (Richard Baxter).

---

[27] Thomas Paine, quoted in Dennis Rainey, "Famous Last Words," *Family Life*, accessed 26 July 2009, https://www.familylife.com/articles/topics/life-issues/challenges/death-and-dying/famous-last-words/.

[28] Ibid.

[29] Dwight L. Moody, quoted in J. Wilbur Chapman, "The Life and Work of Dwight Lyman Moody," accessed 26 July 2009, https://www.biblebelievers.com/moody/27.html.

[30] John Wesley, quoted in Bos, Carole "John Wesley on His Deathbed" AwesomeStories.com. Oct 07, 2013. Jul 23, 2018. http://www.awesomestories.com/asset/view/John-Wesley-on-His-Deathbed.

Hudson Taylor, founder of China Inland Mission, in the closing months of his life, said to a friend, "I am so weak. I can't read my Bible. I can't even pray. I can only lie still in God's arms like a little child and trust."[31]

Sooner or later we will all die. We need to accept this fact without fear. We don't know when it will come, but it will come. How are we going to react? The Bible says there are two destinations: heaven and hell. Where will you spend eternity? C. S. Lewis, the famous Christian author, once said, "The safest road to hell is a gradual one—the gentle slope, soft underfoot, without sudden turnings, without milestones, without signposts. It's that slippery slope that you gradually go down as your life passes by."[32]

So, my question for you is, which road are you on? The road that leads to life eternal with Christ or this slippery slope that finally lands you in hell? The Bible is actually quite clear about what happens after we die. Revelation 20:11–15 says,

> Then I saw a great white throne and him who was seated on it. From his presence earth and sky fled away, and no place was found for them. And I saw the dead, great and small, standing before the throne, and books were opened. Then another book was opened, which is the book of life. And the dead were judged by what was written in the books, according to what they had done. And the sea gave up the dead who were in it, Death and Hades gave up the dead who were in them, and they were judged, each one of them, according to what they had done. Then Death and Hades were thrown

---

[31] Hudson Taylor, quoted in "Last Words of Great Saints," Sermon Index. net, accessed 26 July 2009, http://www.sermonindex.net/modules/newbb/viewtopic.php?topic_id=3933&forum=34.

[32] C. S. Lewis, *The Screwtape Letters* (New York: HarperCollins Publishers, 1942), p. 64.

into the lake of fire. This is the second death, the lake of fire. And if anyone's name was not found written in the book of life, he was thrown into the lake of fire.

The Bible is very clear. There will be a final judgment. I'm sure there will be some on that dreadful day saying, "Hey, hold on a minute. I lived a good life. I was a decent person. I had good morals." But you see, that's just not good enough. Your name must be written in the Lamb's Book of Life. There is only one way to prepare to die, and this is by believing in God's one and only Son, Jesus Christ. God has provided a way of escape to eternal life, but the choice is up to you. Therefore, death for the Christian is tempered with the hope of the resurrection.

So, how about you? Are you prepared to meet God? Are you prepared to die? Will you make your peace with God? Do you know the victory that comes through Jesus Christ? If not, why not settle matters with the Lord right now? You don't have to be afraid of death. The Bible says God loved us so much that He sent His only son to die in our place on the cross. His offer to you is eternal life if you would only trust Him. Let me encourage you right now where you are to pray and commit your life to Him. You might want to pray a prayer similar to this:

> Lord Jesus, I believe that you died on the cross for me and that you were raised from the dead to give me eternal life. I want to turn from my sin and place my faith in you right now. Please come into my life and be my Savior and Lord. In your name I pray. Amen.

Now, if you sincerely prayed this prayer, you can know with assurance Christ promises to come in. You are also assured of eternity with Christ in heaven when you pray and commit your life to Him.

I came across a quote from Martin Luther King Jr. that sums up what I am trying to communicate in this chapter. He shared these words in September 1963, at the funeral for the four little girls who were killed by the bomb blast at Sixteenth Street Baptist Church in Birmingham, Alabama. He sought to bring comfort to those who were gathered together on this sad occasion by saying,

> I hope you can find some consolation from Christianity's affirmation that death is not the end. Death is not a period that ends the great sentence of life, but a comma that punctuates it to more lofty significance. Death is not a blind alley that leads the human race into a state of nothingness, but an open door which leads man into eternal life ...[33]

I read the sad story of a young man who became stranded in an Alaskan wilderness. His adventure began in the spring of 1981, when he was flown into the desolate North Country to photograph the natural beauty and mysteries of the tundra. He had photo equipment, five hundred rolls of film, several firearms, and fourteen hundred pounds of provisions. As the months passed, the entries in his diary, which at first detailed his wonder and fascination with the wildlife around him, turned into a pathetic record of a nightmare. In August he wrote, "I think I should have used more foresight about arranging my departure. I'll soon find out." He waited and waited, but no one came to his rescue. In November he died in a nameless valley, by a nameless lake, 225 miles northeast of Fairbanks. An investigation revealed that he had carefully mapped out his venture, but he had made no provision to be flown out of the area. Have you made arrangements for your departure? Are you ready to meet your Maker?

---

[33] Martin Luther King Jr., "Eulogy for the Martyred Children," 18 September 1963, Birmingham, Alabama, accessed 12 September 1999, https://kinginstitute.stanford.edu/eulogy-martyred-children.

So I'm back to my original questions: Are you afraid to die? Are you so afraid of dying that you have forgotten to live? In these uncertain days, it is comforting to know Jesus has prepared a place for us. You can have victory over death! You do not have to be afraid. Let me close with one other story I often share at funerals. I first heard a pastor share this story several years ago, and it has brought a lot of comfort to me. I hope it will do the same for you.

He began by asking the question, "Do you ever remember going on a long car trip when you were a child? You fell asleep somewhere along the way, and when you got home your father picked you up and placed you in your room. Maybe Mom tucked you into bed, but when you woke up in the morning you were home and you were very happy to be there. This is what death is like for the person who has placed their hope and trust in Jesus Christ. You fall asleep in Christ and wake up at home in heaven." It's graduation, not retribution! It's an inheritance, not penance! It's joy, not sorrow! It's home for all eternity with those who love God and call upon His name.

CHAPTER TEN

🔲🔲🔲🔲🔲🔲🔲🔲🔲🔲🔲🔲🔲🔲🔲🔲🔲🔲🔲🔲🔲🔲🔲🔲

I Want to Go Home

I read about a little boy and his dad who went to the Empire State Building for a visit. They got on the elevator and started to the top. The boy watched the signs flashing as they went by the floors: 10, 20, 30, 40, 50, 60, 70 …. They kept going and going, and he was getting nervous. So he took his father's hand and said, "Daddy, does God know we're coming?" Yes, God knows we are coming, and He has prepared a special place for us. Do you ever think about heaven? Do you ever read your Bible and think about how beautiful it's going to be? Do you ever wish you were there already?

I heard a story about a pastor who went on a study break for a couple of weeks, and someone called the church office wanting to speak with him. The secretary answering the phone said, "I'm sorry. He's not here. He's gone to be with the Lord." There was a long pause, and the secretary realized what she had said, so she quickly added, "But he'll be back next week!"

I'm not getting a load up to go today. And I don't want to go before my time, but heaven really is a wonderful place and I have no hesitation in saying, "I'm looking forward to being there someday." I actually feel like the little boy I read about.

A story is told about a pastor who went out late one summer evening to visit a family from his church. It was starting to get dark when the pastor arrived, but he noticed one of the boys out in the yard holding a string. He walked over and asked the boy what he was doing. He said, "I'm flying my kite." The pastor looked up and said, "I can't see a kite." The boy said, "I can't see it either, but I know it's there, because I can feel the tug." Can you feel the tug? Do you long to go there? I know Christians are sometimes accused of being so heavenly minded they are no earthly good, but I want to share with you in this final chapter five reasons I long for my home in heaven … five reasons why I'm excited about getting to go there someday.

Reason #1: Heaven is characterized by joy instead of sorrow.

Let's begin by looking at the similarities between Isaiah 65:18–19 talking about the New Jerusalem and John's description of heaven in Revelation 21:4.

> But be glad and rejoice forever in what I will create, for I will create Jerusalem to be a delight and its people a joy. I will rejoice over Jerusalem and take delight in my people; the sound of weeping and of crying will be heard in it no more (Isaiah 65:18–19).

> He will wipe every tear from their eyes. There will be no more death or mourning or crying or pain, for the old order of things has passed away (Revelation 21:4).

I'm looking forward to a place where there will be no more pain, tears, crying, suffering, and death. I had the opportunity a number of years ago to speak with a young man who worked as a prison guard at a state prison near Los Angeles. He had the responsibility of watching over some of the vilest, most despicable criminals Los Angeles had to offer. He is not a Christian, and near the end of our conversation he said, "If there is a God, then why does He allow these guys to do all of these horrible things?" This is an excellent question. Why does God allow evil in the world? This question is what tripped my friend up and kept him from faith. It might be a question someone reading this book has stumbled over. Why does God allow evil?

The best answer I can give is that God didn't so much allow evil as he allowed us to have free will, or choice. God could have created us as mindless puppets without the capacity to think and choose, but instead, he gave us the freedom of choice to either worship or reject Him. Sin first entered the world through the disobedience of Adam and Eve, and people have been sinning ever since. We have all sinned and fallen short of God's best for our lives. We live in a fallen, sinful, broken world.

Francis Schaeffer, a famous theologian and philosopher, served Christ faithfully for many years, but near the end of his life, he was struck with terminal leukemia. Someone asked him how he could rationalize the goodness of God and his terminal illness. He said, "Why shouldn't I get cancer? I live in a fallen world and am subject to all the plagues that come with it … The difference is that I know my eternal future, because I belong to Christ."[34]

We praise God with Dr. Schaeffer that our eternal future includes a heaven free from pain, sickness, and disease. It's a place where God will wipe away every tear, a place filled with joy and not sorrows. It's a wonderful place. Can you feel the tug?

---

[34] Frances Schaeffer, quoted in Paul E. Little, *How to Give Away Your Faith* (Downers Grove, Illinois: Intervarsity Press, 1966), pp. 123–124.

MARK S. MILWEE

Reason #2: Heaven is characterized by justice instead of inequity.

Why do babies die, and why are young men cut down in the prime of their lives? These are good questions, and there are no simple answers. Notice what the Bible says in Isaiah 65:20:

> Never again will there be in it an infant who lives but a few days, or an old man who does not live out his years; he who dies at a hundred will be thought a mere youth; he who fails to reach a hundred will be considered accursed.

Ironically, there are those who think they have all of the answers. They say things like, "Well, God just needed another flower for His garden," or "He was too good for this world, so God took him on home." But somehow, when this happens to you, these answers seem horribly trite, shallow, and inconsiderate. It makes a person want to say, "If God wanted another flower for His garden, then let Him take somebody else's baby," or "If the only reason my husband is in heaven is because he was so good, then I wish he hadn't have been so good!" No, the truth is that there is real pain and real heartache in this world. There is real grief. And if you live long enough, one of these days it's going to come knocking on your door, and no amount of well-intentioned talking will make it go away.

The good news is that it's not always going to be like this. We actually are going to a much better place. Jesus says in John 16:33, "I have told you these things, so that in me you may have peace. In this world you will have trouble. But take heart! I have overcome the world."

And in John 14, Jesus proclaims,

> Do not let your hearts be troubled. Trust in God; trust also in me. In my Father's house are many

rooms; if it were not so, I would have told you. I am going there to prepare a place for you. And if I go and prepare a place for you, I will come back and take you to be with me that you also may be where I am" (John 14:1–3).

We live in a world of injustice and inequity, but we worship a Savior who has overcome this world. He has prepared a better place for us, and someday He is going to come and take us there to be with Him. Therefore, we should have the attitude of a little boy I read about who was dying of AIDS. He had been infected with the virus at birth from his mother, but he lived for several years. He was a bundle of energy, and his mother often told him she needed to dress him in red so she could quickly spot him when he was out playing with his friends. Finally, the disease caught up with him, and his mother tried to bring him comfort by telling him she also had the disease, and she would also be dying soon. A few days before his death, he called one of the nurses over to his bed and whispered, "I might die soon. I'm not scared. When I die, please dress me in red. My mom promised that she's coming to heaven too. I'll be playing when she gets there, and I want to make sure she can find me."[35]

As Christians, we don't have to fear death, because we know and understand we are going to a much better place, a place where Christ himself has gone before and prepared for us. He has prepared it just for you! Can you feel the tug? So, heaven is characterized by joy not sorrow, justice not inequity, and now the third reason I'm longing for heaven is because heaven is characterized by fulfillment, not emptiness.

---

[35] Jack Canfield and Mark Victor Hansen, *A 3rd Serving of Chicken Soup for the Soul: 101 More Stories to Open the Heart and Rekindle the Spirit* (Deerfield Beach, FL: Health Communications Inc., 1996), p. 177.

Reason #3: Heaven is characterized by fulfillment instead of emptiness.

In Isaiah 65, beginning with verse 21, we read,

> They will build houses and dwell in them; they will plant vineyards and eat their fruit. No longer will they build houses and others live in them, or plant and others eat. For as the days of a tree, so will be the days of my people; my chosen ones will long enjoy the works of their hands. They will not toil in vain or bear children doomed to misfortune; for they will be a people blessed by the LORD, they and their descendants with them (Isaiah 65:21–23).

In today's world, we often hear the statement, "Americans are the loneliest people on earth." This is ironic considering all of our advances, all of our gadgets, and all of our opportunities, and yet people are still looking for meaning and fulfillment in their lives. People are longing for relationships. People are searching for opportunities to make their lives count for something. I'm amazed at how hard some people work just to have more possessions. But once we acquire more "stuff," we discover these things provide little or no lasting satisfaction. I remember an old country song that came on the radio when I was a kid. This was long before country music became cool. We would hear this song, and I remember just howling in laughter with my cousins. The chorus of the song went, "Work your fingers to the bone—what do you get? Bony fingers! Bony fingers! Bony fingers!"

The children of Israel found themselves in a similar situation. They worked hard all of their lives to build their homes, plant vineyards, and raise their children, but now they found themselves in exile, captives in Babylon, and a long way from home. Can you imagine how wonderful these words must have sounded to their ears? God had not forgotten them. God had not rejected them. God had not abandoned them. Their labor was not in vain. Jesus says the same to us in Matthew 11:28: "Come to me, all you who are weary and burdened, and I will give you rest."

One of the key characteristics of heaven will be rest and fulfillment that is found only through a personal relationship with Jesus Christ. I can't wait to get there! Can you feel the tug? Now, reason number 4 is …

Reason #4: Heaven is characterized by answers instead of questions.

Do you have any questions you want God to answer? I don't know about you, but I sure do. Isaiah 65:24 brings comfort when it states, "Before they call I will answer; while they are still speaking I will hear." Job was a man with many questions. In Job 30:20 he exclaims, "I cry out to you, O God, but you do not answer; I stand up, but you merely look at me."

Do you feel like this sometimes? I know I do. This is why Paul writes in 1 Corinthians 13:12, "Now we see but a poor reflection as in a mirror; then we shall see face to face. Now I know in part; then I shall know fully, even as I am fully known."

I like what Max Depree once said about questions. He states, "We do not grow by knowing all of the answers, but rather by living with the questions."[36]

There are just some things we will never know until we get there, and I'm very comfortable with that. I like how Steven Curtis Chapman puts it when he writes,

> I have learned that we can control where we allow
> things that we can't understand to fall. They either
> fall between us and God, and we become angry. Or

---

[36] Max DePree, "Leadership Is an Art," *Leadership Journal*, (1989) vol. 15, no. 3.

we allow these things to fall outside of us and press us in closer to God.[37]

So, are your questions pushing you farther away from God, or are they pressing you in closer to Him? In heaven, we will discover all the answers. I can definitely feel the tug! Now, we come to the final reason I'm longing for my home in heaven.

Reason #5: Heaven is characterized by peace instead of fear.

We live in a world filled with talk about war and rumors of war, which reminds us again that we live in a sinful, fallen world. But God's word reminds us there is no fear in heaven:

> "The wolf and the lamb will feed together, and the lion will eat straw like the ox, but dust will be the serpent's food. They will neither harm nor destroy on all my holy mountain," says the LORD (Isaiah 65:25).

There will be no pain, no sorrow, no suffering in heaven. The lion and the lamb will lie down together. Heaven is characterized by peace, and this peace is found only through a personal relationship with Christ. Revelation 22:10–13 says,

> Then he told me, "Do not seal up the words of the prophecy of this book, because the time is near. Let him who does wrong continue to do wrong; let him who is vile continue to be vile; let him who does right continue to do right; and let him who is

---

[37] Stephen Curtis Chapman, "Steven Curtis Chapman's Silent Nights," *Christian Reader* (March/April 2002), p. 59

holy continue to be holy. Behold, I am coming soon! My reward is with me, and I will give to everyone according to what he has done. I am the Alpha and the Omega, the First and the Last, the Beginning and the End."

Now, skip down to verse 17:

The Spirit and the bride say, "Come!" And let him who hears say, "Come!" Whoever is thirsty, let him come; and whoever wishes, let him take the free gift of the water of life (Revelation 22:17).

I was up late one night. It was the night before Rebekah, our oldest daughter, would be leaving to go back to college. I was reminiscing with her about some of our favorite memories. One of my best memories of her is from when she was very little and I would come home from work. She would come running and jump up in my arms, give me a great, big hug, and scream, "Daddy!" It's one of the joys of having small children. I cherish those memories, but the Bible gives us a very different portrait. In the story of the prodigal son, in Luke 15, we see a similar, but different, scenario playing out. Listen and see if you can discern the difference:

So he got up and went to his father. But while he was still a long way off, his father saw him and was filled with compassion for him; he ran to his son, threw his arms around him and kissed him (Luke 15:20).

Did you notice the difference? The father is running to greet the son! Can you imagine God the Father running to welcome you into heaven someday? He's going to. He's going to be right there to welcome you home. That is, if you have made your preparations to go. Can you feel the tug? Is Christ tugging at the door of your heart today? I don't know when your time will come. I don't know when my time will come, but I'm longing to go. I can feel the tug. How about you?

CLOSING COMMENTS

I began writing this book with one primary purpose in mind. I wanted to help people see and understand the value senior adults bring to the life of the church. They are a valuable asset to any church and deserve to be valued, cherished, and treated with dignity and respect. We are clearly taught in the word of God to respect the elderly and defer to their wisdom. We are also taught to remember our leaders and imitate their faith. Therefore, we are foolish when we discount their wisdom and shortsighted when we do not understand their value.

However, as I got more and more into the book, I also wanted to help seniors understand that respect must be earned instead of demanded. We have to be careful not to display a sense of entitlement, and insist our way is the only way. We have the opportunity, during our twilight years, to be either a blessing or a hindrance to the Lord's work. We can make the decision to grow old gracefully. I hope I have issued a clear challenge to every senior reading this book to be a blessing to everyone around you. As Oscar Wilde once famously said, "Some people bring happiness wherever they go; others whenever they go." We want to strive for the former and avoid the latter. You have it within your power to be a tremendous force for good to everyone in your life.

Finally, in the later chapters of this book, I sought to bring comfort to those who are facing death in the near future. As Christians, we have nothing to fear, because our Savior has gone before us and prepared a place for us. My favorite illustration of this truth comes from Anne Cetas, writing in *Our Daily Bread*. She shares Henry van Dyke's beautiful description of dying. I think it is one of the most touching descriptions of death I have ever read. He wrote,

> I am standing at the seashore. A ship at my side spreads her white sails to the morning breeze and starts for the blue ocean. I stand and watch her until at length, she hangs like a speck of white cloud, just where the sea and sky come to mingle with each other ... And just at the moment when someone at my side says: "There, she is gone!" there are other eyes watching her coming, and other voices ready to take up the glad shout: "Here she comes!" And that is dying.[38]

Anne adds, "Even more comforting for the loved ones of a believer who dies, are the words of the apostle Paul: 'If our earthly house, this tent, is destroyed, we have a building from God, a house not made with hands, eternal in the heavens' (2 Corinthians 5:1). We can rejoice in our sorrow knowing our departed loved ones are now present with the Lord." God's word assures us, "Precious in the sight of the LORD is the death of His saints." (Psalm 116:15) It also adds, "Brothers, we do not want you to be ignorant about those who fall asleep, or to grieve like the rest of men, who have no hope. We believe that Jesus died and rose again, and so we believe that God will bring with Jesus, those who have fallen asleep in him."[39] We grieve, but not as those who have no hope. Our hope is in the LORD Jesus Christ, and in the future reserved for those who put their faith and trust in Him. Therefore, let me close where we started with the beautiful words of Robert Browning:

---

[38] Henry van Dyke, quoted in Randy Alcorn, *Heaven* (Carol Stream, Illinois: Tyndale House Publisher's Inc., 2004), p. 352.

[39] Anne Cetas, "A Sailing Ship," *Our Daily Bread*, 24 April 2008, accessed 15 May 2009, https://odb.org/2008/04/24/a-sailing-ship/.

Grow old along with me!
The best is yet to be,
The last of life, for which the first was made:
Our times are in his hand
Who saith, "A whole I planned,
Youth shows but half; trust God: see all, nor be afraid!"